Hugo Münsterberg on Film

**The Photoplay:
A Psychological Study**

and Other Writings

Edited by
ALLAN LANGDALE

Routledge
New York   London

Published in 2002 by
Routledge
29 West 35th Street
New York, NY 10001

Published in Great Britain by
Routledge
11 New Fetter Lane
London EC4P 4EE

Routledge is an imprint of the Taylor & Francis Group

Library of Congress Cataloging-in-Publication Data

Hugo Munsterberg on film : The photoplay—a psychological study and other writings / edited by Allan Langdale.
    p. cm.
  Includes bibliographical references and index.
  ISBN 0-415-93706-X — ISBN 0-415-93707-8 (pbk.)
  1. Motion pictures.   I. Langdale, Allan.

PN1994.M8 2001
791.43—dc21
                                                 2001019641

Contents

Contents

Additional Writings and Texts

Acknowledgments

There have been several people who encouraged me in my plan to offer a new edition of Hugo Münsterberg's *The Photoplay: A Psychological Study.* My first exposure to the text was several years ago in Edward Branigan's film theory class at the University of California at Santa Barbara, and Edward's energetic promotion played a central role in the realization of the project. Similarly, Constance Penley has for many years advocated my interest in film studies, and Chuck Wolfe helped greatly with his support during my search for a publisher. Edward Branigan, Chuck Wolfe, Melinda Szaloky, Lisa Parks, and Dore Carter lent invaluable advice during the editing process, and I am very thankful for their efforts.

I would also like to thank William Germano for embracing the proposal and making it possible for a new generation of film scholars and students of the history of psychology to have access to *The Photoplay* and to these supplementary writings of Hugo Münsterberg. Joe Palladino deserves mention for his kind encouragement, while Chris Husted can be credited with applying unrelenting pressure on me to undertake the reissue. They all have my sincere gratitude.

I am indebted to the staff of the Special Collections department of the Boston Public Library who were generous with their Münsterberg archive materials. I would also like to extend thanks to Frank A. J. L. James of the Royal Institution for assisting me with an important reference and the mysterious web-based personage "Mr. X," who tracked down another article I had trouble locating. The book could not have been completed without the kindness of Suzanne and Reece Duca and the unwavering support of my mother, Nancy. Finally, I would like to thank the students of the film studies department at UCSB, who have been a source of continual energy and inspiration.

S(t)imulation of Mind:
The Film Theory of Hugo Münsterberg

Allan Langdale

> ... films have the appeal of a presence and of a proximity that strikes
> the masses and fills the movie theaters. This phenomenon, which is
> related to the impression of reality, is naturally of great aesthetic sig-
> nificance, but its basis is first of all psychological.[1]
>
> —Christian Metz

In July of 1930 Welford Beaton published an article provocatively
titled "In Darkest Hollywood" in *The New Republic*. In it he enthusiastically champions a book, published 14 years before, which sadly
seems to have already disappeared from sight:

> Neither in the main Hollywood library nor in any of its branches can
> a copy of this book be found. It is not for sale in a Hollywood book-
> store. I have not encountered a dozen people who have read it, or
> two dozen who have heard of it. The film industry is one of tremen-
> dous proportions, yet this great contribution to its mentality is out
> of print.[2]

The great contribution Beaton was referring to was *The Photoplay: A
Psychological Study*, written by one of the leading figures in the field
of psychology, Hugo Münsterberg.[3]

Forty years after Beaton's lament, in the introduction to the 1970
Dover reprint of Münsterberg's book, Richard Griffith also noted the
book's disappearance.[4] One could write those same words of Beaton's
today, but in the thirty-one year interim since the Dover edition there
has been modest but significant attention devoted to Münsterberg in

1

general and to *The Photoplay* in particular.[5] The book is regarded by many to be the first serious piece of film theory, and is one of the first books to argue for the potentialities of film as an independent art form.[6] Few would dispute its important place in the history of film theory. Yet this significant piece of early film theory has been largely unavailable to the current generation of film students and scholars—to say nothing of students of psychology and philosophy for whom this book should also hold substantial interest. It is with this in mind that we have published a new edition of *The Photoplay* along with a number of supplementary writings by Münsterberg on film, none published in English after their original appearance in the years 1915 to 1917.[7] Included is an interview as well as a speech by Münsterberg[8] and a piece entitled "Why We Go to the Movies," which is an excursion into film that prefigures *The Photoplay*.[9] Another article, "Peril to Childhood in the Movies," deals with the issue of the effects of film violence on children. This essay not only reflects attitudes towards film violence in the early 20th century, but is a revealing expression of Münsterberg's social idealism.[10] Also included is the section on *The Photoplay* from Margaret Münsterberg's 1922 biography of her father, an admiring remembrance composed by a daughter attempting to record a definitive and positive portrayal of a man America had since turned its back upon.[11]

Today, relatively few people in the disciplines of film studies or psychology know very much about Hugo Münsterberg and yet around 1915 he was probably the most famous academic in the United States. His books were widely read and his ideas discussed in broad circles.[12] One of the first students of the emerging school of experimental psychology in his youth, Münsterberg later distinguished himself as the founding father of applied psychology.[13] Münsterberg is well known for his books and articles on the subject, including *Vocation and Learning* (1912), *Psychology and Industrial Efficiency* (1912), *Business Psychology* (1915), and *Psychology: General and Applied* (1916).[14] He developed psychological tests to help the Boston Elevated Railway Company find the least accident prone drivers for their trolleys, and composed similar experiments for the Hamburg American Shipping Company to test for those persons who would make the best ship captains.[15]

To place *The Photoplay* in a historical and biographical context, some details of Münsterberg's life and career should be considered.[16] Hugo Münsterberg was born in Danzig in 1863, the son of a Jewish lumber merchant, Moritz Münsterberg, and his second wife Anna. He had two older brothers, Otto and Emil—who had been born to Moritz's previous wife, Rosalie—and one younger brother, Oskar.[17] The family's central tragedies were the deaths, first, of Rosalie, then of Anna in 1875 when Hugo was twelve years old. This loss, according to Phyllis Keller in her largely psycho-biographical account of Münsterberg's life, had profound effects on his personality and attitudes.[18] He developed a great desire to please his father—perhaps in consolation for their mutual loss—but he also developed a fear of abandonment and rejection, a fear that, as we shall see, was ultimately realized on a grand scale later in his life. His early education was eclectic and ranged between arts and sciences; he studied languages, music, wrote stories and poetry, and was interested in archaeology, botany, and read widely in literature. In the years after the death of his father in 1881, Münsterberg adopted a strident nationalism and began to idealize the role of culture in the perfecting of German society.[19] He also embraced scholarship and increasingly began to identify himself with academic success, being the only one of the Münsterberg sons to complete his *Gymnasium* training and to pass his *Abitur* examinations, thus opening the door to an academic career.[20] Along with his two younger brothers, Münsterberg was baptized shortly after the death of his father; a decision, as Matthew Hale notes, that was not at all uncommon in German society in the late 19th century since adhering to one's Judaism could severely curtail a young man's institutional ambitions, including attending a university.[21]

Münsterberg's academic training began in 1882 with the study of medicine in Leipzig where, in the summer of 1883, he heard lectures by the major figure in German experimental psychology, Wilhelm

3

Wundt. It was then that Münsterberg's previously disparate interests found a passionate focus.[22] He began a doctoral program with Wundt in 1885 and produced a thesis on "The Doctrine of Natural Adaptation."[23] After completing an M.D. at Heidelberg, Münsterberg progressed through the ranks of academia with his assignment as a *Privatdocent* at the University of Freiburg in 1887.[24] Just after his 28th birthday in 1892, he was elected *extraordentlicher Professor*, the equivalent of a tenured professor.

At Freiburg Münsterberg displayed unparalleled enthusiasm for psychological experimentation and took the unprecedented initiative of setting up an experimental laboratory in his home at his own expense. Soon thereafter Münsterberg produced, in astonishingly rapid succession, the early texts which would win him an international reputation: *The Activity of the Will* (1889), *Contributions to Experimental Psychology* (1889), and *Aims and Methods of Psychology* (1891).[25] With these volumes Münsterberg established himself as a force in the new field of experimental psychology. Equally important was that the positions taken in these books situated Münsterberg in opposition to his former teacher, the great Wundt, thus demonstrating Münsterberg's independence as a scholar.[26] While alienating Wundt's numerous devotees, he simultaneously gained the admiration of other psychologists who questioned Wundt's tenets, most notably the premiere American psychologist, William James, who had called Münsterberg's *Activity of the Will* "a little masterpiece."[27] A fateful meeting of the two men occurred in 1889 at the First International Congress of Psychologists in Paris. It was there that James's positive evaluation of Münsterberg's work was augmented by an equally enthusiastic appraisal of Münsterberg the man, and this would lead James to invite Münsterberg to join the faculty at Harvard for a three year period between 1892 and 1895.

The sojourn at Harvard was one of the most enjoyable times of Münsterberg's life. He established strong personal and academic friendships and his scholarship and teaching were respected by the Harvard community. He returned to Freiburg in 1895 with an offer of a permanent position at Harvard and a two-year period in which to consider it. Even though Münsterberg cherished the notion of a prestigious chair in a German university the offer from Harvard proved irresistibly attractive and in the fall of 1897, at the age of 34, he arrived in Cambridge with his family, furniture, and substantial library to take up his post as Professor of Experimental Psychology.

Münsterberg's fame grew steadily during his years in America, but so too did his notoriety, and he never regained the contentment of his earlier stay.[28] Although beginning peacefully enough, his American career gradually soured until, at the time of his death nineteen years later, he had suffered numerous humiliations and had endured the painful ostracism of his Harvard colleagues and those in American society whose friendship and support he had earlier enjoyed.[29] Nor was history Münsterberg's ally. From the start of his American years the psychologist had situated himself as an apologist for Germany and German culture. At the same time, he became an unrelenting critic of American society. Münsterberg, split between an idealization of his German homeland and his life in America—"a German who has pitched his tent among the Americans," as he put it in the preface to *American Traits*—took it upon himself to explain America to Germans while also pointing out the faults of America to Americans. These authoritarian observations, starting in 1901 with *American Traits from the German Point of View*,[30] continued with *The Americans* (1904), *American Problems from the Point of View of a Psychologist* (1910), and *American Patriotism and other Social Studies* (1913). In these volumes Münsterberg did not disguise his partiality towards German *Kultur* and his disdain for the American way of doing things.[31] Münsterberg also became the major spokesperson for German Americans, a considerable body of individuals with significant economic and political influence. So intimately involved and infused with Germany and German culture, Münsterberg's position became increasingly precarious as American relations with Germany gradually deteriorated, eventually leading to U.S. entry into World War I.[32]

Part of this decay in advocacy also had to do with Münsterberg's own mandarin-like personality, which alienated him from those who had earlier offered support. Frank Landy notes that, "The difficulties caused by Münsterberg's pro-German attitudes and behavior were compounded by his personal style. He was condescending to all but Germans.... No criticism, real or imagined, was ignored. His rebuttals were petulant, sarcastic, and long."[33] Numerous issues irritated his colleagues. For example, despite his earlier criticism in *American Traits* that American academics wasted their time becoming popularizers of their disciplines, Münsterberg himself became glaringly guilty of this very practice.[34] Similarly, Münsterberg's aggressive involvement in political affairs, which ranged from writing impassioned letters to Presidents Roosevelt and Wilson and Kaiser Wilhelm to publishing an article against prohibition, deflected him from his professorial duties and made him unpopular with the American public.[35]

After 1910 Münsterberg rapidly lost his allies. William James, the moving force behind bringing Münsterberg to America, was gradually estranged by Münsterberg's sense of entitlement and his mocking attacks on the "psychological" performances of mystics and spiritualists, persons whose displays of "mental phenomenon" James took very seriously.[36] This pattern of alienation was repeated with many of Münsterberg's friends, yet the event that finally severed any remaining threads of sympathy was not of his doing. History intervened to annihilate his hopes, and, indeed, the hopes of many German-Americans who longed for good German-American relations despite the hostilities in Europe. In May of 1915 a German U-boat sank the British passenger vessel *Lusitania*, resulting in the deaths of 1,198 civilians, 124 of whom were American. Overnight American attitudes toward Germans slid from suspicion to vilification. It must have seemed to Hugo Münsterberg that by the years 1914-1915 he was a man who had lost many things that were important to him: his mother at 12, his father at 18, his Judaism at 22, his country at 34, and his valued collegial respect by middle age.[37]

Some time in 1914, for some inexplicable reason—but perhaps for mere escapism or out of curiosity—a likely despairing Hugo Münsterberg went to a moving picture for the first time in his life.

The movie was *Neptune's Daughter*, a fantasy film directed by Herbert Brenon and starring Annette Kellerman.[38] The story had the epic qualities of the fantasy literature Münsterberg loved to read and write as a boy. In it, the daughter of King Neptune, a mermaid, travels to dry land to avenge the death of her sister who was accidentally killed by a fishing net cast by William, the King of the Terrestrial Kingdom. However, she falls in love with the very man whom she had come to avenge herself upon. Back in her watery world, aided by an army of mermaids, she does battle with the Witch of the Sea. Perhaps this story reminded Münsterberg of the fables he wrote as a child when his mother was still alive and actively encouraged him in such imaginative and creative explorations. In his childhood tale, "The Pearls," there is a battle for a Queen of the Forest, while in other juvenilia he revealed a fascination with myths of Baltic mermaids.[39] It may be that the fortuitous personal resonance of this particular film sparked Münsterberg's passion for the medium, bringing him back, even if momentarily, to the fond memories of his childhood which contrasted so markedly with his present, embattled situation in adult life.

Whatever the effects, it is nonetheless true that Münsterberg launched himself with great enthusiasm into the study, and later even the modest production, of films.[40] The writing of *The Photoplay* may also have been spurred by Münsterberg's desire to embrace America's most popular art form as a way of endearing himself to the average American who had every reason at this point to dislike him. In "Why We Go to the Movies" the hauteur of the earlier writings is replaced by a meeker, confessional tenor. One discerns him trying to soften the image of the elitist, teutonic professor:

> I may confess frankly that I was one of those snobbish late-comers. Until a year ago I had never seen a real photoplay. Although I was always a passionate lover of the theater, I should have felt it as undignified for a Harvard professor to attend a moving picture show, just as I should not have gone to a vaudeville performance or to a museum of wax figures or to a phonograph concert. Last year, while

7

> I was traveling a thousand miles from Boston, I and a friend risked
> seeing *Neptune's Daughter,* and my conversion was rapid. I recog-
> nized at once that here marvelous possibilities were open, and I
> began to explore with eagerness the world which was new to me.[41]

Nonetheless he still presents himself as the expert observer, carefully
guiding the unenlightened reader through his analysis of the film
medium. This attitude, though less emphatic, also permeates *The
Photoplay,* in which Münsterberg states that the expert psychologist
is able to offer deep insights into the art of the moving pictures. In
this respect, *The Photoplay* can be seen to be closely related to
Münsterberg's numerous publications in applied psychology in which
he extended a hand to business and manufacturing in order to promote the role of psychology in the aid of industrial efficiency.[42] When
researching *The Photoplay* he claims, in "Why We Go to the Movies,"
to have immersed himself in the workings of the industry.

> I went with the crowd to Anita Stewart and Mary Pickford and
> Charles Chaplin; I saw Pathé and Vitagraph, Lubin and Essanay,
> Paramount and Majestic, Universal and Knickerbocker. I read books
> on how to write scenarios; I visited the manufacturing companies,
> and, finally, I began to experiment myself.

This was at a time when the movie production companies would have
greatly appreciated the intellectual attention of a famous professor
and psychologist, for it was in these years that the industry was
attempting to make more "high brow" films that would appeal to
more sophisticated, middle and upper class audiences. This shift called
for more feature length films and less emphasis on short-format,
Nickelodeon programs.[43] This redirection in the industry's production
meant that sustained, coherent story-telling became more and more
central to the medium. The *Photoplay,* in many respects, can be read
as a response to these impulses, and Münsterberg's book was a welcome legitimization, especially since it argued for film as an independ-

ent and sophisticated art form. It should be mentioned, however, that in *The Photoplay* Münsterberg operates as a philosopher as much as a psychologist, and this stems in part from the close relationship between the two disciplines in the early part of the century.[44] While playing the psychologist in articulating the ways in which film operates like the human mind, Münsterberg also gives considerable attention to ontological and aesthetic questions pertaining to art in general and film in particular. Thus his philosophical position on film was closely linked to his general philosophy of art.

As we read Münsterberg's book armed with the benefit of hindsight and 85 years of film theory—Arnheim, Bazin, Kracauer, Metz, Baudry, Mulvey, and others—it is at times difficult not to read *The Photoplay* as a series of missed opportunities. We are used to a kind of sophistication and rigor Münsterberg does not always deliver. Yet Münsterberg's ideas warrant serious attention not only from a historical perspective but from contemporary film theorists who are interested in the psychology of the cinematic spectator. Münsterberg was the first film theorist to seriously argue for the film medium as a model of the workings of the human mind, a paradigm later elaborated by, for example, Christian Metz and Jean-Louis Baudry. Noël Carroll has pointed to the inherent faults in film-mind analogies, yet such analogies cannot be summarily rejected, if only because they form a major part of the history of film theory.[45] While Münsterberg stands as a precursor—perhaps somewhat ironically, since he did not even believe the unconscious existed—of film theorists working in the psychoanalytic paradigm (Metz and Baudry), Münsterberg is also a crucial figure for theorists who are challenging that tradition. As Pasi Nyyssonen notes, Münsterberg takes on added currency at this moment when a "cognitive turn" is occurring in contemporary film theory. Moreover, recent scholarship on the formation and role of emotions in narrative encourages us to look anew at Münsterberg's contributions.[46] The questions that we typically ask of a theorist's work yield crucial information about Münsterberg's thoughts on the medium. What is his attitude towards reality, authorship, spectatorship, the camera, the screen, the

9

frame, the shot, film sound, color, and so on? Such investigation can also lead us to fruitful comparisons to other film theorists.[47]

Münsterberg's book is situated in a provocative and singular moment before two world wars forever changed western philosophical ideas and social attitudes towards media, technology, and the nature of the "subject." While some might dismiss the book and its author as nineteenth-century holdovers, it is perhaps for this very reason that *The Photoplay* should be of great interest to us. Not enough has been made of *The Photoplay* being a lone theoretical voice from this early age of cinema.[48] In arguing for film as a new art form, Münsterberg seems to be aware that the medium heralds a new way of perceiving the world. He realizes that the visual and visuality have forever been altered by the advent of the moving picture. We may find some of Münsterberg's conclusions questionable, but we must admit that he was often asking the right kinds of questions. Today, confronted with a plethora of new media and interactive apparatuses, it would be profitable to revisit Münsterberg's basic line of inquiry and to consider new ways of analyzing and reworking his film theory.

It would also be rewarding to consider *The Photoplay*'s relationships to Münsterberg's other psychological and philosophical theories. Donald Fredericksen did this when he considered Münsterberg's philosophy of art in *The Photoplay* against the backdrop of Münsterberg's *Eternal Values* and the concept of aesthetic isolation articulated therein.[49] Numerous other possibilities await attention, including examining Münsterberg's theories of applied and experimental psychology and the relation between media and mind in *The Photoplay*. Münsterberg's notions about the psychology of advertising would be relevant to such an account, as would be his general theory on the function of culture.[50] Another possible avenue of research is Münsterberg's attitude toward the dangers of film to a youthful audience, as this might be compared with either contemporary or contemporaneous anxieties about film and its threat to morality and the social order. Similarly, while numerous scholars have analyzed the intellectual impact of émigrés from Europe during World War II

(Siegfried Kracauer, Theodor Adorno, and so on), much less attention has been given to émigrés from around the time of World War I, and one could justifiably include Münsterberg in such a study.[51] Recent interest in William James and the currents of American Pragmatism and Functionalism, and the history of experimental psychology in general, offer new possibilities for a re-examination of Münsterberg's oeuvre, *The Photoplay* included. Indeed, there are many provocative paths to follow from Münsterberg's book, only a few of which can be suggested here. In what follows I introduce some of the major issues in *The Photoplay* and try to demonstrate some of their correlations with Münsterberg's general psychology and philosophy. An attempt has also been made, if all too cursorily, to suggest ways in which Münsterberg's film theory provocatively resonates with other film theories.

The Photoplay begins with an introduction divided into two parts, one called "The Outer Development of the Moving Pictures" and the other explaining "The Inner Development of the Moving Pictures." In the first, Münsterberg gives a history of the evolution of the scientific inventions that contributed to the evolution of early cinema, including the psychological innovators who examined the perceptual mechanisms involved in the impression of movement.[52] In the second, the inner, artistic developments are traced. The division between the two is indicative of Münsterberg's desire to emphatically segregate the world of mechanical apparatuses from the purely artistic, inner world of film. Since Münsterberg will quickly abandon this "outer," technical world in favor of the artistic elements of film, he becomes one of the first of many theorists to relegate the cinematic apparatus to an invisible or, at least, secondary position in the consideration of the medium. Like many of the early film theorists, Münsterberg is primarily interested in focussing on film as an art form.

An explanation for Münsterberg's dual organization of inner and outer developments lies in a section of his volume *Art Education* in which he makes a distinction between "Connection in Science and Isolation in Art."[53] For Münsterberg, science examines the ways in which things are interconnected in the world, how nature is a vast machine of interrelated components. The scientist, as well as the social scientist or historian, gives us an account of causes and effects, of how these elements act upon one another. Since science only describes the connections between things, it offers no real insight or truth about *the thing in itself.* Münsterberg believed that science "leads us away from the object we are interested in, leads us away to other objects with which it may be connected."[54] How, then, do we know the things *in themselves?* He answers with his description of aesthetic "isolation":

> Thus if you really want the thing in itself there is only one way to get it: you must separate it from everything else, you must disconnect it from causes and effects, you must bring it before the mind so that there remains no room for anything besides it. If that can ever be reached, the result must be clear: for the object it means complete isolation; for the subject, it means complete repose in the object, and that is complete satisfaction with the object; and that is, finally, merely another name for the enjoyment of beauty. To isolate the object for the mind, means to make it beautiful . . . [55]

Art objects or art forms are things most congenial to this process for they have been specifically designed for the purpose of aesthetic contemplation. Thus we find that Münsterberg's early division of the cinema into "outer" and "inner" developments parallels a dichotomy consistent with his general philosophy of knowledge. The historical and mechanical overview of the first section demonstrates the technical causes of the scientific progress of the early cinema—its outer, scientific development—while the remainder of the book focuses on the inner, artistic and aesthetic aspects of the medium.

"The Inner Development of the Moving Pictures" draws a distinction between the non-fictional and fictional or narrative film. Münsterberg has enthusiasm for the informational films that record daily life, political events, or sporting events; or those that display the wonders of nature or far off lands.[56] Despite his respect for this type of film, Münsterberg sees it as a mere supplement to the truly important sort of moving picture, that is, the narrative fiction film produced for mass entertainment.[57] By using the term "entertainment," however, Münsterberg is not being dismissive. Instead he asks a serious question about the medium: "What was the real principle of the inner development on this artistic side?" In response to his own query, Münsterberg gives an evolutionary history of narration that structurally parallels his earlier review of the progression of technical apparatuses. At first, moving pictures were enjoyable simply because they showed the illusion of movement, and that in itself was fascinating and entertaining. "But soon," Münsterberg writes, "touching episodes were staged, little humorous scenes or melodramatic actions were played before the camera, and the same emotions stirred which up to that time only the true theater play had awakened." Here Münsterberg begins a critical strategy that will characterize the rest of *The Photoplay*, a comparison between the live stage drama and the moving picture. In this, Münsterberg becomes the first of several major film theorists who seriously discuss the differences between film and theater as a way to clarify their ontologies of cinema, Siegfried Kracauer, Béla Balázs and Jean Mitry among them.[58]

Münsterberg observes that many critics thought the moving picture to be a poor imitation of the live theater. This may have been true early on, Münsterberg says, but the moving pictures began to develop narrative and dramatic techniques that were impossible in the theater. For example, while the theater may seem more real because live people are appearing before the spectator, film can set its narratives in the "real" world, not bound by the painted backdrops of the live theater, which betray the stage's own ample share of artifice. These differences between film and stage help set up the question central to his book:

> The art of the photoplay has developed so many new features which have not even any similarity to the technique of the stage that the

13

question arises: is it not really a new art which long since left behind the mere film reproduction of the theater and which ought to be acknowledged in its own aesthetic independence?

Münsterberg sees two avenues by which to consider the question, one psychological and the other aesthetic. He casts a psychologist's eye on the physiology, perception, and mental functioning of the spectator, while the philosopher in him considers the intrinsic aesthetic qualities of the art and the emotions and moral attitudes that the medium can elicit and engender.

Having broadly laid out the issues of film's relation to reality, the human mind, and its status as an independent art in the introduction, Münsterberg's divides his first chapter into the categories of "Depth and Movement," "Attention," "Memory and Imagination," and "Emotions." These subjects are arranged in a hierarchical fashion from lower to higher perceptual and mental processes. The simple perception of depth and movement stand at one end, while the stirring of human emotion occupies the more evolved and complex pole of mental activity. The first of these sections, "Depth and Movement," takes up the issue of the impression of dimensionality and the illusion of motion. He begins by stating that, even though we *know* that film is two-dimensional, it is not our *impression* that it is so:

> It is flat like a picture and never plastic like a work of sculpture or architecture or like a stage. Yet this is knowledge and not immediate impression. We have no right whatever to say that the scenes which we see on the screen appear to us as flat pictures.[59]

Münsterberg becomes the first of numerous theoreticians, André Bazin and Christian Metz among them, to note the strong impression of reality in the cinema, and to argue that this is a crucial part of its psychological effects. He observes that even when we close one eye, the strong impression of the world's three-dimensionality does not disappear. There are many depth cues that still operate in the absence of stereoscopic vision—such as overlapping, diminution of size, and other perspective relations communicated through composition—and all of these are at work in the film image. Münsterberg suggests that the spectator take up a position in the movie theater which takes full advantage of the perspectival constructions of the photograph. Using the idea of the cinematic screen being like a glass plate over the face of a stage, Münsterberg proposes that film, for all intents and purposes, is a window onto the world. He writes: "If the pictures are well taken and the projection is sharp and we sit at the right distance from the picture, we must have the same impression as if we looked through a glass plate into a real space."[60] Such proposals warrant attention, for Münsterberg here demonstrates an acute awareness of the cinematic viewing apparatus and how being in the "center" of it facilitates the medium's effects, something dealt with in greater detail by such later film theorists as Jean-Louis Baudry.[61]

Münsterberg also indulges in a complex excursus on the perceptual illusions pertaining to movement. The modern psychologist, according to Münsterberg, has much to say about this issue. For instance, there are times when we perceive movement when no movement is taking place. Such tricks of perception may seem to have little to do with the illusion perpetuated by the moving pictures—indeed they have no direct bearing[62]—but Münsterberg identifies these problems in order to illustrate a vital concept: since we cannot be sure that movement *really* takes place in objective reality, the perception of movement may well be mental, an operation of the mind. Such is exactly the case in film. When watching the movements of actors on the real stage the movement is correctly perceived as continuous movements of bodies in real space. Movement *really* happens in the objective outer world. However in film, the movement is *created* by the mind, by the afterimages which our perceptual apparatus provide us when the pictures are rapidly shown to us. So here too, as with depth, it is not an absolute *reality* of space or motion but *our mental perception of it* that makes film particularly well-suited to "picturing" the inner workings of the mind.

Such concerns should not surprise us in the theoretical investigations of a psychologist since one of the features of perception that typically interest psychologists are optical illusions. Münsterberg was no exception, and he is credited with the discovery of some new illusions such as "The Münsterberg Checkerboard Illusion."[63] Optical illusions throw perception into question, they prove that perception, at least in some cases, is a mental act and has only a partial relationship to "reality." This is entirely consistent with Münsterberg's theory of mind. Theorists and philosophers such as Kant and Leibniz, and Münsterberg's teacher Wundt after them, believed that the mind peremptorily *acted upon* the data that came in through the perceptual apparatuses. Thinking *predetermined* the perception of the objects of the world. Münsterberg reversed this. He believed that the primary stimulus for mental activity came from perception. One saw or heard something, *then* the mind responded to and manipulated it.[64] Film, like any other thing to be perceived by a viewer, was sensory data upon which the mind could work after the perceptive stimulus was received. Matthew Hale has noted the correlation between Münsterberg's theorized cinema spectator and Münsterberg's "Action Theory" of mind. The mind, Hale writes, participated

> ... in the creation of its perceptions, but it did not do so spontaneously. It was simply a reactive mechanism more reactive than that of the associationists. Münsterberg valued film not because it allowed more creativity on the part of the audience, but because it permitted more control by the artist over the aesthetic experience.[65]

We find significant concordance here with Sergei Eisenstein's early notions about the intimate, yet unidirectional connection between film and mind. While Eisenstein was informed by Pavlovian theories, Münsterberg's theory of mind similarly seems to suggest a behaviorist point of view: simply, the film provides the stimulus and the spectator responds.

But the stimulus is only the beginning of a complete perceptual act. Münsterberg addresses the concept of "Attention" beginning with a clear demarcation between the lower processes of the perception of depth and movement and the higher mental process of attention: "The mere perception of the men and women and of the background, with all their depth and their motion," Münsterberg writes, "furnishes only the material." Perception is "mere" and supplies "only the material," that is, *only* the base stimulus for mental activity. With the act of attention we are brought to a more sophisticated mental operation. The chaos of the material of the outer world is made manageable for us by the selectivity of our mind. Münsterberg draws an important distinction here between voluntary and involuntary attention.[66] We might voluntarily listen to a bird sing, but a backfiring car may demand our involuntary attention. In one, the impetus comes from within the mind, while in the other the stimulus comes from an external source. Works of art engage our involuntary attention. We may choose to go to the theater, but when the play begins the actors and settings attract our attention through speech, lighting, backdrops and so on.[67] We surrender our attentiveness to the work of art and allow it to orchestrate how and when we concentrate. Here too we find mute resonances with Eisenstein, whose early theory of a "montage of attractions" explains the ways in which the spectator's attention is drawn and directed by the film medium.[68]

It is clear that the live stage directs our sight and hearing through the speech and movements of the actors. How does this compare, Münsterberg asks, with the moving pictures? The silent film lacks the spoken word, yet this, Münsterberg contends, is in fact an aspect of its strength, for we are made to concentrate even more closely on the gestures and expressions of the actors. But the most important parallel of attention in the moving pictures, one that contrasts it dramatically the theater, is the close-up. We may indeed have our attention drawn to an actor's hand on the stage, but "that dramatic hand must remain, after all, only the ten thousandth part of the space of the whole stage." In contrast film can utilize a close-up of that hand, bringing it to the center of our consciousness. "Here," Münsterberg declares, "begins the art of the photoplay." Details of the visual world of the film, whether they be objects, subjective points of view, or expressions, may be emphasized by the close-up, which "heightens the vividness" of the object and mirrors the act of attention.

"Attention" is a master concept in virtually all of Münsterberg's psychology but it is especially prominent in his work in applied psychology. This should come as no surprise. In attempting to discern the aptitude of particular workers, the manner in which they attend to the task is a crucial aspect of their ability to complete it. He writes,

> The problem of attention, indeed, seems to stand quite in the center of the field of industrial efficiency. This conviction has grown upon me in my observation of industrial life. The peculiar kind of attention decides more than any other mental trait for which economic activity the individual is adapted.[69]

Münsterberg was an expert on the vicissitudes of human attention. He was interested in the nature of its various permutations and applications, its duration and how it fatigued, was fixed, or wandered. For some workers, the ability to pay attention to a very confined object or repetitive movement without tiring was paramount. In other cases a natural ability to redirect one's attention to movement in the periphery of vision was desirable.[70] Münsterberg also believed that an individual's sensory array was remarkably consistent. He claims that his laboratory experiments demonstrated that when a particular person is, for example, good at attending visually to a very small and discrete object, they are very likely to be able to attend acoustically to an almost inaudible sound.[71] In other words, Münsterberg saw attention to be a primary marker. As the most fundamental of the sensory and mental elements, it determined the nature of the higher mental attributes of the individual. So too does the manipulation of attention serve as a primary and definitive attribute of film art.[72]

As with the attention and the close-up, "Memory and Imagination" can be used in ways impossible in the theater. Although theater actors may reminisce about something they remember, we are limited to listening to their recitations. Film, mirroring the mind's ability to visualize, can show us the memory itself. The flashback, or "cut-back" as Münsterberg calls it, also provides insight into the mind of the character, articulating an experience of remembering that the live drama cannot express. Similarly, the flash forward closely matches the operation of imagining something in the future, just as the subjective insert gives us unparalleled access to the dreamy imaginings of a human mind. Dramatic possibilities are thus multiplied by the fluid transitions which can keep pace with the kind of visualizing our own minds are capable of.[73] Clearly, one of the reasons Münsterberg saw film as an extraordinary "medium of the mind" is that the mind has to do so little with the stimulus since the medium simulates mental structures so accurately. The ease of the transmission of data is made possible because the medium is already disposed in the way that the mind already "works."

Memory is tempered, sometimes in positive and sometimes in negative ways, by another concept that crops up in Münsterberg's chapter on memory and imagination—suggestion. In Münsterberg's work on forensic psychology, suggestion is a subtle but powerful stimulus which can severely compromise the accuracy of memory.[74] When Münsterberg considers suggestion in the context of advertising, he proposes ways in which advertisers can use graphic design, words, and other strategies to plant positive suggestions and associations in the minds of prospective clients.[75] In *The Photoplay*, Münsterberg describes the difference between an imagined and a suggested thought. He notes that suggested thought is similar to imagination in that it is controlled by the play of associations. But there is a crucial difference. When imagining objects or persons our associations are our own, and these are "felt as our subjective supplements." The suggestion, on the other hand, though also felt as our own, is a stealth-thought which comes from an external stimulus organized so as to instigate specific associations, taking their place like intruders alongside the associations that really do spring from our own minds.

A suggestion, on the other hand, is forced on us. The outer perception is not only a starting point but a controlling influence. The associated idea is not felt as our creation but as something to which we have to submit.

Suggestion is a powerful psychological element (hypnotism providing the extreme case) and Münsterberg notes too that the moviegoer is "certainly in a state of heightened suggestibility and is ready to receive suggestions." Provocative though these observations are, Münsterberg does relatively little with them in this section of *The Photoplay* and reduces his complex notion, analyzed more deeply in some of his other writings, to a simple narrative device where the action is begun in a shot but is cut off before its completion, leaving the completed action as an implanted suggestion in the viewer's mind. He gives as an example a girl undressing, where the shot ends before the final garment is discarded, providing the suggestion of what will happen next. The viewer is obliged to imagine the completion of the action and picture her nakedness mentally. More insidious possibilities for suggestion in film, dealt with momentarily, are alluded to at the end of *The Photoplay* when Münsterberg considers the possibility of the moral corruption of youth by film. Yet even then he fails to see, in his own model, that all film is essentially "suggestion." Again our minds may turn to the early Eisenstein, whose early model of the cinematic spectator was similar in spirit.[76]

Münsterberg also deals with the highest of the mind's operations, emotion. Arrival at this elevated platform is signaled by the first line: "To picture the emotions must be the central aim of the photoplay." A stage actor's speech may hold our attention but photoplay actors, in their world of silence, must always be soliciting our emotions through facial expression, gesture and action.[77] But the human body is only part of the expressive arsenal of the moving pictures. Setting, too, can play an important role in evoking emotions. The settings must have a spiritual unity with the narrative, not simply providing realistic places for action, but reinforcing the emotions elicited by the action. The filmmaker has unlimited possibilities, not only in the variety of locations offered by nature but by the way several sites can be alternated, allowing for swift and dramatic shifts in both setting and emotion. Münsterberg also makes note of suspense, a powerful element in cinematic narrative. With almost Hitchcockian succinctness he observes that we are more effectively aroused if we see a child playing near a steep precipice when the child is unaware of the danger.

In "The Aesthetics of the Photoplay" Münsterberg presents his general theory of art and how the moving pictures fit into that theory. He begins by assailing the notion that art imitates nature. Art is bound to reality in many ways, yet it is precisely the distance of representation from reality that makes something art. Figures in a wax museum may recreate a personage in a very convincing fashion, yet we do not value these as art as we do the colorless marble images of ancient Greece. Münsterberg argues that art does not really imitate reality, but instead re-presents a portion of it, transformed, to the spectator.

> Wherever we examine without prejudice the mental effects of true works of art in literature or music, in painting or sculpture, in decorative arts or architecture, we find that the central aesthetic value is directly opposed to the spirit of imitation. A work of art may and must start from something which awakens in us the interests of reality and which contains traits of reality, and to that extent it cannot avoid some imitation. *But it becomes art just in so far as it overcomes reality, stops imitating it and leaves the imitated reality behind it.* [Münsterberg's italics][78]

A work of art is not primarily mimetic, but rather a creation which instigates an aesthetic experience, and the hallmark of the aesthetic experience is the beholder's feeling of *perfect isolation*. Why is this something to be valued? Münsterberg replies with an almost disarmingly simple answer: "Might we not answer that this enjoyment of the artistic work results from the fact that only in contact with an isolated experience can we feel perfectly happy?" Münsterberg sees this as art's beauty, where all the parts of the work point only to the expression of the work itself in a harmony and simplicity which resonates with and back upon itself, unconnected and unburdened by reference or direct connection to the outer world. The spectator, drawn into the vortex of perfect isolation, is thus also segregated from the vagaries of real existence to enjoy, in "inexhaustible happiness," the harmoniousness of the work of art.[79] Vaunted, even romanticized though this theorized spectator may at first seem, Münsterberg's viewer may also be justifiably described as an automaton responding thoughtlessly to the powerful stimulus of the motion picture. Similar to the consumer in Münsterberg's work on advertising, or the laborer in his books on industrial efficiency, the theatergoer is a passive entity whose mentality can be subtly manipulated by external stimuli.

Like many early theorists who adopted purist arguments when advocating film as an art, Münsterberg contends that film's strengths lie in the specific techniques that distinguish it from other arts. These medium-specific characteristics should be exploited to maximum effect and should not be supplemented by attributes shared by other media. The dramatic manipulation of time and space in the photoplay is its natural manner of telling a story, taking us into the past (memory) and the future (imagination), and freely and creatively breaking the space-time continuum. Film should embrace these possibilities as enthusiastically as the stage drama, bound to its own physicality, should avoid them.[80] Even though Münsterberg's position on artistic purity echoes many similar such debates on the nature of different arts, the paradigm takes on a provocative resonance since it also so closely parallels nineteenth and early twentieth-century theories of industrial efficiency: find the most efficient way of manufacturing something, and build a machine that does only that thing and does it the best. Münsterberg himself was a pioneer in extending that logic to the worker: use psychological testing to find the best person for a particular job and have them do the thing they do best. When everyone is doing the thing they are best suited to do, this will contribute to social harmony. The fetish of efficiency in labor, a central concern of Münsterberg's, finds its counterpart in his aesthetics of film: find out what the medium of film does best and have it do only those things—this will lead to a "good" film product. Good films will in turn lead to the aesthetic education of the masses and, ultimately, to a better society.

In step with his philosophy of the purity of film art, Münsterberg was against the use of synchronous film sound. Experiments using the phonograph to create simultaneous speech were, according to Münsterberg, precipitated by inventors like Edison who had scientific but not aesthetic interests in mind. Efforts to synchronize sound to the film image, Münsterberg suggests, were bound to fail since they were ill conceived from an aesthetic perspective. Speech was a threat to the visual authenticity of the medium. Sound effects which imitate the clopping of horses' hooves, the rumble of lightning, or the shot of a gun were gimmicks, mere "appeals to the imagination" which "have no right to existence in a work of art that is composed of pictures."[81] However Münsterberg, somewhat at odds with his purist aesthetic attitude, is not so dismissive of non-diegetic music. Here, he seems to take a pragmatic position. Citing the boredom of the audience during the long projection of a photoplay, he writes that "The music relieves the tension and keeps the attention awake." This rather surprising shift in aesthetic disposition also finds its explanation in Münsterberg's work on industrial productivity. One of the most deleterious effects on a worker's productivity was fatigue, to which Münsterberg devotes an entire section of *Psychology and Industrial Efficiency*.[82] In this section of *The Photoplay* we find Münsterberg alternating between being a philosopher championing the purity of the art form and a pragmatic psychologist interested in the efficiency of the film medium. A film cannot be effective if the audience's attention is allowed to waver, and music helps keep the spectator alert.[83]

In the penultimate section, "The Demands of the Photoplay," Münsterberg considers the notion of the film artist, an issue of some interest in the history of the evaluation of film as an art. He lays out a definition of the "photopoet" and mere stager of film scenarios which to some degree resembles the distinction between *auteurs* and *metteurs-en-scène* in modern criticism. In further articulating his idea of the film artist, Münsterberg singles out two main contributors to the film, the "scenario writer" and the "producer" (whose role appears equivalent to our sense of the director today[84]), the "two inventive personalities" who must work together to make a successful film. But they are by no means equal contributors. Münsterberg feels that the film script is different than a play script or a musical score. The latter are works of art even before they are performed by actors or musicians. But the photoplay script does not become a work of art *until* it is realized on the screen, translated to the film medium *by the producer/director*. The role of a film producer is thus entirely different than that of a stage manager for a play. The stage manager is presented with a piece of literature, a work of art in its own right, and his duty is to present that play in a fashion dictated by and faithful to the dramatic text. This situation is reversed in film. The film producer elevates the scenario writer's story into a complete work of art through a process of creative adaptation. Since the film writer works with words, and words are largely missing from the film medium, the writer cannot be considered the primary artist, or even *an* artist, in film production. The producer is responsible for the images which convey the story and emotions of the film, and thus is the sole and true "artist" of the film medium. He is the "photopoet." In short, film is *visual*. It *pictures* emotions. A script is only a preliminary story guide for the *filming* of the work, where the true artistic process happens.[85]

The final section of the book is an account of both the social benefits and dangers of film. The concerns Münsterberg raises here—and in the posthumously published "Peril to Childhood in the Movies" included in this volume—have a contemporary ring. He begins by reminding his readers of the astonishing numbers of people who attend the moving pictures and he worries about the powerful effects that cinema may have on these spectators. The strong parallels with the working of the human mind, which Münsterberg has championed as positive features of film, are also the very aspects that make it necessary to attend to its influences on susceptible spectators. In comments that strongly prefigure popular sentiments about film violence today, Münsterberg observes that

> The sight of crime and of vice may *force itself on the consciousness* with disastrous results. The normal *resistance breaks down* and the moral balance, which would have been kept under the habitual stimuli of the narrow routine life, may be lost under the pressure of the *realistic suggestions*. At the same time the subtle sensitiveness of the young mind may suffer from the rude contrasts between the farces and the passionate romances which follow with benumbing speed in the darkened house. The possibilities of *psychical infection* and destruction cannot be overlooked. [my emphases]

The entranced viewer, fascinated by the spectacle of the moving pictures, is potentially threatened by the medium's powerful effects.[86] Precariously balanced between reality and unreality, the spectator can experience the aesthetic isolation of a work of art, but may just as easily have his or her moral senses undermined by the scenes of violence or vice which typify films "of low moral standard." It is here where the notion of "suggestion"—indeed, "psychical infection"—takes on the more provocative overtones alluded to earlier. In the "darkened house" images flash with "benumbing speed," bringing to mind a passive and fascinated spectator at the mercy of the apparatus. "Realistic suggestions" force themselves on the consciousness of viewers, breaking down their "normal resistance." Even while his rhetoric echoes contemporaneous general observations about the dizzying and disorientating effects of the medium, Münsterberg's nonetheless displays uncommon sensitivity to the powerful effects of the situation of viewing film. This is as close as Münsterberg get to recognizing the implications of the passive spectator he has theorized throughout. Yet here, as in all his writings, he fails to confront the subject he creates: a blank screen upon which the world of the senses is projected. It is when we consider this aspect of Münsterberg's theory that we see that the film screen is equivalent to the human mind and our ocular equipment parallel to the impassive camera. Film is more like the mind than Münsterberg himself was willing to admit. Light sensations come into our eyes and our minds sort out basic perceptual cues like depth and movement, then process the stimuli through attention, and the associations of memory and imagination, resulting in an emotional response. Münsterberg reveals himself very much a man of his time with a model that is at once organic and mechanical, seeing no contradiction between the two.

Even though Münsterberg expresses concern over the possible negative influences of the photoplay, in the end he is far more convinced of its positive social potential. Münsterberg saw education in aesthetics as the primary social role of all the arts, film included, and he believed that aesthetic education had positive ethical and social effects. Photoplays of good quality would improve not only the aesthetic sensibilities but the morality of Americans. This attitude follows from Münsterberg's German Idealist stance on the role of culture in the evolution of society. Matthew Hale states the case well:

> The photoplay, therefore, did not derive its value from its purely diversionary qualities. National in scope and popular in appeal, it provided a new and unifying source of inspiration and self-discipline. It offered the possibility—it seemed—of extending for a while to ordinary people the peace and passivity that art had always instilled in the cultivated.[87]

The photoplay was thus a democratic art that could take its place among the other civilizing arts, each in its proper place, efficiently exercising its specific aesthetic functions to the social benefit of all. Münsterberg's vision of a maturing art form is full of hope. He wonders "whether a Leonardo, a Shakespeare, a Mozart will ever be born for it." At a time when the world must have seemed to be unraveling—and when he may well have known his health was failing (he would be dead within a year, of a cerebral hemorrhage while lecturing at Radcliffe), Hugo Münsterberg was able to optimistically champion, "a new form of true beauty in the turmoil of a technical age, created by its very technique and yet more that any other art destined to over-come outer nature by the free and joyful play of the mind." Even though we have already seen that there was little real hope of the mind being free and playful in Münsterberg's model, in his ardency we might be reminded of another German theorist, 19 years later and near death himself, who, amidst the horrors of World War II, tried to find a revolutionary and liberating hope in the aura-destroying features of the medium of film.[88]

NOTES

1.   Christian Metz, "On the Impression of Reality in the Cinema," chapter in *Film Language: A Semiotics of the Cinema*, trans. Michael Taylor (New York: Oxford University Press, 1974), 5.

2.   Welford Beaton, "In Darkest Hollywood," *The New Republic* 63, n. 816 (July 23rd, 1930): 287–289.

3.   Hugo Münsterberg, *The Photoplay: A Psychological Study* (New York: D. Appleton & Co., 1916).

4.   Griffith notes that after World War I people wanted to forget their poor treatment of Münsterberg in the pre-war years and thus repressed both the memory of the man and of *The Photoplay*. I have given a more detailed account of the public attitude towards Münsterberg during this time. See Griffith introduction, pp. ix–xi. The Dover edition, under a modified title, was a reprint of the 1916 publication: Hugo Münsterberg, *The Film: A Psychological Study. The Silent Photoplay in 1916* (New York: Dover Publications, 1970). In the same year, Arno Press, New York, came out with an exact reprint with the same title as the original, with no supplementary introduction or forward. In 1977 Merle Moskowitz wrote that *The Photoplay* had "been reissued a number of times." I am unaware of editions other than the ones I have mentioned here. See Merle Moskowitz, "Hugo Münsterberg. A Study in the History of Applied Psychology," *American Psychologist* 32, n. 10 (Ocotober, 1977): 838.

5.   In this introduction I have included references to much of this work in the notes.

6.   *The Photoplay* is clearly more compelling than Vachel Lindsay's book on film which appeared the year before Münsterberg's: Vachel Lindsay, *Art of the Moving Pictures* (New York: MacMillan, 1915). Lindsay wrote two letters to Münsterberg, both regarding mutual support for each others' contributions to film. These letters are kept in the Münsterberg archives in the Boston Public Library. They are dated May 3rd, 1916 and May 26th, 1916 [ref. MSS Acc. 1899]. Lindsay also wrote a review of *The Photoplay* the year after Münsterberg's death. See Vachel Lindsay, review of Hugo

Münsterberg's *The Photoplay: A Psychological Study*, in *The New Republic* (Feb. 17th, 1917): 76–77. For a comparison of the outlooks of the two authors see Michael Pressler, "Poet and Professor on the Movies," *The Gettysburg Review* 4, n. 1 (Winter, 1991): 157–165. A survey of the early contributors to American film criticism, including Münsterberg and Lindsay, can be found in Myron Osborn Lounsbury's *The Origins of American Film Criticism 1909–1939* (New York: Arno Press, 1973).

7. During the course of researching this project I found that I was not the first to come up with the idea of reissuing *The Photoplay* with additional writings on film by Münsterberg. An Austrian, German language edition of *The Photoplay* with other writings by Münsterberg appeared in 1996. Edited, translated, and with an introduction by Jörg Schweinitz, the volume is entitled *Hugo Münsterberg: Das Lichtspiel. Eine psychologische Studie (1916) und andere Schriften zum Kino* (Wien: SYNEMA-Publikationen, 1996). See reviews of the volume by Peter Wuss, *Weimarer Beiträge* 43, n. 2 (1997): 310–313; and Pasi Nyyssonen, "Film Theory at the Turning Point of Modernity," *Film-Philosophy: Electronic Salon*, 17 October 1998, http://www.mailbase.ac.uk/lists/film-philosophy/files/nyyssonen.html.

8. The interview was with a reporter from Paramount Pictures and took place on April 25th, 1916. There are two versions of this interview, one a transcript on typewritten pages in the Boston Public Library, Münsterberg Papers [MS Acc. 2461]; and the modified, published version which appeared as "Psychology of the Photoplay," in *The New York Dramatic Mirror*, 75, n. 1954 (June 3, 1916). The version published here is from the Boston Public Library transcript. The original transcript has been chosen in part because Münsterberg himself distrusted the manipulative rewritings of reporters and journalists, expressing his views in "The Case of the Reporter," *McClure's Magazine* 36, n. 4 (February, 1911): 435–438. Münsterberg's speech was on his contributions to the Paramount Pictographs: "Münsterberg Speaks at Paramount Reception," *Motography* 15, n. 22 (May 27, 1916): 1215.

9. Hugo Münsterberg, "Why We Go to the Movies," *Cosmopolitan* 60, n. 1 (Dec. 15, 1915): 22–32.

10. Hugo Münsterberg, "Peril to Childhood in the Movies," *Mother's Magazine* 12 (Feb. 12th, 1917): 109–10 and 158–59.

11. Margaret Münsterberg, *Hugo Münsterberg: His Life and Work* (New York: D. Appleton & Co., 1922). The erasure of Münsterberg's memory is best exemplified by the group portrait of the founding fathers of the Harvard department of Psychology, in which there is a blank space rumored to be where the image of Münsterberg was painted over.

12. Münsterberg was the author of numerous books and articles, including the best-selling *On the Witness Stand. Essays on Psychology and Crime* (New York: Doubleday, 1909). This book had been preceded by a series of popular articles all published in *McClure's Magazine*: "Nothing But the Truth," *McClure's Magazine* 27, n. 4 (August, 1907): 532–536; "The Third Degree," *McClure's Magazine* 29, n. 6 (October,

1907): 614–622; and "Hypnotism and Crime," *McClure's Magazine* 30, n. 3 (January, 1908): 317–322. These publications established Münsterberg as one of the first forensic psychologists. Münsterberg also gained sensational notoriety when he used a chronoscope and word associations to test the veracity of Harry Orchard, the murderer of the Idaho union leader Frank Steunenberg. Orchard was to implicate another labor leader, Big Bill Haywood, in the scheme. Münsterberg, taking a very unpopular position, claimed that his tests validated Orchard's damning testimony. See Matthew Hale Jr., *Human Science and Social Order. Hugo Münsterberg and the Origins of Applied Psychology* (Philadelphia: Temple University Press, 1980), 116–119. Hale's authoritative volume is the best single source on Münsterberg's life and ideas.

13. For Münsterberg's contributions to philosophy and psychology, see the previously cited Moskowitz, "Hugo Münsterberg: A Study in the History of Applied Psychology," 824–42; and sections from Bruce Kuklick's *Rise of American Philosophy: Cambridge Massachusetts, 1860–1930* (New Haven: Yale University Press, 1977), 196–214 and 435–447.

14. These were augmented by articles in popular magazines such as "Psychology and the Market," *McClure's Magazine* 34, n. 1 (November, 1909): 87–93; and "Finding a Life Work" *McClure's Magazine* 34, n. 4 (February, 1910): 398–403.

15. Hale's chapter 10, "Industrial Efficiency," in *Human Science*, pp. 148–163, is an excellent account of Münsterberg's theories of Applied Psychology. The chapters in question, on trolley operators and ship captains, are found in Hugo Münsterberg, *Psychology and Industrial Efficiency* (Boston & New York: Houghton Mifflin Co., 1913), 63–82 and 83–96 respectively.

16. For more detailed biographical accounts of Münsterberg's life—and ones that my synopsis is indebted to—see the previously cited Matthew Hale Jr., *Human Science*; Jutta and Lothar Spillmann, "The Rise and Fall of Hugo Münsterberg," *Journal of the History of the Behavioral Sciences* 29, n. 4 (October, 1993): 322–338; Frank J. Landy, "Hugo Münsterberg: Victim or Visionary?," *Journal of Applied Psychology* 77, n. 6 (December, 1992): 787–802; Phyllis Keller's chapter on Münsterberg in her *States of Belonging: German-American Intellectuals and the First World War* (Cambridge, Mass., and London: Harvard University Press, 1979); and the previously cited Margaret Münsterberg, *Hugo Münsterberg: His Life and Work*.

17. In order to prevent confusion for researchers, it should be noted that Oskar Münsterberg named one of his sons Hugo, and that Hugo Münsterberg became a well known art historian with many publications, particularly on Asian art. He was a professor at the State University of New York New Paltz and died in 1995.

18. Münsterberg had been very close to his mother and understandably idealized his happy childhood with her, most notably memories of her in the garden of the family home in Langfuhr. Keller, *States of Belonging*, 10. Although the psycho-biographical element is strong in Keller's volume, she nonetheless offers considerable insight into the intellectual history and social situation of Münsterberg's life.

19. Keller writes: "Some years after his father's death, Hugo became not a cosmopolitan German but an earnest nationalist and patriot. Significantly, he later defined the German national character in a way congruent with his Jewish upbringing. It, too, developed from a system of values that stressed rules, regulations, and injunctions to obey the law regardless of reason or pleasure. Thus Hugo retained the form while eschewing the content of his father's moral universe." Ibid., 16. Still, one need not insist too strongly on Münsterberg's patriotism being linked to the loss of a father figure. It was, after all, a time of enthusiastic and pervasive patriotism in Germany, linked far more firmly to social and historical factors than to individual, family dramas.

20. Matthew Hale, in comments complimenting Keller's above, noted the nature of the educational system of the *Gymnasium*: "The pursuit of cultivation within the *Gymnasium* was autocratic, rigidly intellectual, and self-consciously humanistic. The curriculum stressed mastery of Latin and Greek as well as extensive familiarity with French, history, and mathematics." Hale, *Human Science*, 17.

21. Ibid., 19. Münsterberg adopted Lutheranism as his new religion, making his conversion as "German" as possible.

22. See the account in Keller, *States of Belonging*, 21–22.

23. Ibid., 23. See also Spillmann and Spillmann, 322–3. Münsterberg claimed that Wundt had directed his studies away from his chosen thesis topic on the nature of human will (Hale, *Human Science*, 22). Nevertheless, Münsterberg later did write on the topic of the will in his book *Die Willenshandlung*.

24. A *Privatdocent* was an unsalaried lecturer who was paid directly by his students. It was a typical interim rank before attaining the higher status of professor (see Hale, *Human Science*, 22). Just before taking his position at Freiburg, Münsterberg had married Selma Oppler, a friend of the family whom Hugo had known since his childhood days at the house in Langfuhr. Like his mother, Selma was artistic and dabbled in painting. This similarity, along with the association of Selma with those halcyon days in Langfuhr, no doubt reminded the young scholar of his mother (see Hale, *Human Science*, 22; and Keller, *States of Belonging*, 23).

25. The original German titles of these volumes are, respectively, *Die Willenshandlung, Beiträge zur experimentallen Psychologie*, and *Aufgaben und Methoden der Psychologie*.

26. The critical reception to Münsterberg's work in Germany was at that moment somewhat negative as Wundt's students and admirers responded strongly to Münsterberg's challenges. Hale, *Human Science*, 23 and Keller, *States of Belonging*, 22–25. See also the comments on the opposition between Wundt's Structuralism and James' Functionalism in Landy, "Hugo Münsterberg, Victim or Visionary," 788.

27. Keller, *States of Belonging*, 23; Landy, "Hugo Münsterberg, Victim or Visionary?", 789.

28. Hale and Keller both give more extensive examinations of the personal, social, and political setbacks of Münsterberg in America. See also Landy, "Hugo

Münsterberg, Victim or Visionary?", 795–6; and Spillmann and Spillmann, "The Rise and Fall of Hugo Münsterberg," 327–334.

29. For the decaying of the relationship between Münsterberg and William James, see Spillmann and Spillmann, 327–8.

30. Of *American Traits* Hale writes: "Despite its insights, there are built in biases and distortions of emphasis throughout the book, the effect of which is to play to Germany's strengths and America's weaknesses." Hale, *Human Science*, 36. Discussion of this and other related volumes can be found on pages 31–38. For Münsterberg's specific critique of American academia see pp. 39–40.

31. One of Münsterberg's most striking, though certainly not unique, evaluations of American society concerned the role of women. For Münsterberg, the increasingly equal position of women—he might have said dominant position—was a sign of America's feminization and this he contrasted with the more virile and "masculine" aspects of German culture. Münsterberg saw the family unit as a microcosm of society and the state, and at the head of the family stood the father. The loss of control of fathers, and the desire of women to escape the duties of the family to become involved in society, led to "an effemination of the higher culture, which is antagonistic to the development of a really representative national civilization." (*American Traits*, as quoted in Hale, *Human Science*, 62). See also Münsterberg's chapter "Women" in *American Traits*. As Hale also notes on his page 63, such accounts of American society were common in America at the time, and President Roosevelt even took the time to write to Münsterberg supporting and echoing his sentiments. For an in-depth analysis, see Rena Sanderson's "Gender and Modernity in Transnational Perspective: Hugo Münsterberg and the American Woman," *Prospects* 23 (1998): 285–313. In 1913 Münsterberg also angered feminists with his assertion that women should be exempted from jury service. He had done psychological tests which determined, he contended, that women's memories were unreliable.

32. For a contemporaneous reply to Münsterberg's opinions on the hostilities in Europe, see John Cowper Powys, *The War and Culture: A Reply to Professor Münsterberg* (New York: G. A. Shaw, 1914). Perhaps thankfully, Münsterberg didn't live to see America's entry into the war.

33. Landy, "Hugo Münsterberg, Victim or Visionary?", 795.

34. Keller, *States of Belonging*, 39–40. Hale provides this quote from the psychologist Lightner Witmer: "The clarion voice of Münsterberg which has been ... heard crying his psychological wares in the marketplace has cheapened the profession of psychology" (See Hale, *Human Science*, 110).

35. After the anti-prohibition piece it was revealed that a German-American beer company had awarded Münsterberg substantial funds for his laboratory, thus undermining Münsterberg's credibility. Others charged that Harvard's Germanic Museum had been the beneficiary of a $50,000.00 gift from the Busch brewing company as a reward for Münsterberg's stand against prohibition (see Keller, *States of Belonging*,

53). Reading the piece today it seems quite correct and reasonable. A reply to Münsterberg's piece was published by Joseph Henry Crooker, *Münsterberg on Moderate Drinking* (Boston: Universalist Publishing House, 1908).

Münsterberg's propensity for involving himself in various political imbroglios was noted with some displeasure by Harvard's president Charles W. Eliot. Keller quotes the following from Eliot's letter in the Münsterberg archives in the Boston Public Library: "What I wish, and what the Corporation wish, is that you should give over your efforts as a special agent or advisor of German authorities about American affairs, or of American authorities about German affairs; that you should limit your activities to your professional and literary work ... [and] cease to communicate on your own initiative with German officials" Ibid., 57. "Later," Keller writes, "after the outbreak of war in Europe, relations between the two men turned to open and bitter hostility" Keller, 59. Münsterberg was tagged as being one of "The Kaiser's American Agents" in an article so-titled in the *London Times* (Saturday, September 26th, 1914): 3. Münsterberg wrote an essay in defense the following year: "The Impeachment of German-Americans," *The New York Times Magazine Section* (September 19th, 1915): 1–2. Münsterberg also often found himself lampooned in newspaper cartoons when he expressed unpopular ideas, something he would have found particularly disrespectful and humiliating. Elsewhere, he was referred to as "Professor Hugo Monsterwork." Still, one could at least say that the public was fascinated with him—a man they loved to hate, as it were.

36. Spillmann and Spillmann, 327–8. An accessible account of Münsterberg's views on spiritualism and mysticism can be found in his "Psychology and Mysticism," *Atlantic Monthly* 83, n. 495 (January, 1899): 67–85. His most sensational piece, sarcastically entitled "My Friends the Spiritualists," was an exposé of Mme. Eusapia Palladino, a famous Italian medium (see Keller, *States of Belonging*, 42–43). It was this article, in a 1909 volume of *Metropolitan Magazine*, which infuriated James, who strongly advocated the study of psychic phenomenon. It was reprinted in Münsterberg's *American Problems*, pp. 122, 142–3. For James's views see George William Barnard, *Exploring Unseen Worlds: William James and the Philosophy of Mysticism* (Albany: State University of New York Press, 1997).

37. There were numerous calls for Münsterberg's resignation. One wealthy alumnus offered Harvard a huge sum of money with the proviso that Münsterberg be fired. Harvard declined the likely insincere offer. Nevertheless, many voiced support for the dismissal.

38. Released April 25th, 1914 by Universal Pictures. The picture is apparently lost and plot synopses are sketchy. The picture, though costly for the time, was financially very successful and was followed in 1916 by a similar aquatic saga called *Daughter of the Gods*, also starring the *Neptune's Daughter* star, Annette Kellermann. Kellerman herself was an interesting figure. An Australian girl who had learned swimming and water sports to help her cope with childhood polio, she became a swimming

star and is known as the first woman to wear a one-piece swimsuit which she herself invented (she was arrested in Boston for wearing it in 1907). She is also known as the founder of synchronized swimming, and the progenitor of that rarified genre of Hollywood films involving aquatic spectacles. Her more famous understudy, Esther Williams, later starred as Kellerman in *Million Dollar Mermaid*, a story based on Kellerman's life, and a 1949 remake of *Neptune's Daughter* starring Williams and Red Skelton.

Merle Moscowitz offers an alternative story about Münsterberg's initiation into the world of film. She claims that Münsterberg's interest in the motion pictures stemmed from a play, "The Third Degree" (inspired by Münsterberg's article and chapter in *On the Witness Stand*) that had in turn been made into a film (see Moscowitz, "Hugo Münsterberg: A Study in the History of Applied Psychology," 838). Jorg Schweinitz notes that Münsterberg's friendship with Hans Heinz Ewers, who was a movie fanatic, may have also encouraged his interest (see Schweinitz, 13).

39.   Keller, *States of Belonging*, 19; Hale, *Human Science*, 17 and 144. Hale suggests that Münsterberg's interest in "The Pearls" focussed on the nobility of service to the "good" Queen, which paralleled Münsterberg's devotion to the ideals of the German State.

40.   Münsterberg's first product was an article published in the popular magazine *The Cosmopolitan* entitled "Why We Go to the Movies," which is included in this volume. It is a piece as interesting for its page layout—complete with several pictures of Münsterberg sitting in his laboratory, visiting the Vitagraph and Pathé film company sets, and talking with the actress Anita Stewart—as it is for its ideas about the medium of film. The article presents, in nascent form, several of the concepts that would form the body of *The Photoplay*, which may in fact have already been completed by this time.

Münsterberg's involvement with actual film production—which seems to have been limited to sketching out the scenarios—came with his contributions, entitled "Testing the Mind," to a series called the "Paramount Pictographs: the Magazine for the Screen" (see a transcript of an interview regarding these in this volume). These were film shorts that preceded feature films in movie theaters. Unhappily, no one has yet managed to find actual copies of Münsterberg's films, which included titles such as *Can You Make Quick Estimates?*, *Are You Quick to Discover a Principle?*, and *Can You Judge Well What is Beautiful and What is Ugly?* However, some documentation, including Münsterberg's own scripts and advertisements in *Moving Picture World*, survive. Sketches of the scenarios of these pieces, presumably typed by Münsterberg himself, may be found in the Münsterberg Papers of the Boston Public Library's Special Collections [MS Acc. 2443]. Münsterberg also mentions his undertakings in film in a letter to a Mr. Samuel McClintock dated September 28th, 1916, also in the Münsterberg Papers in Boston [MS Acc. 2357]. He writes: "In order to popularize the ideal of mental tests and to stimulate the public interest last year I constructed scenarios for moving pictures which allowed everyone in the audience to take part in the tests. The Paramount Pictures Corporation brought them out with unusual success. As two million people have seen those tests on the screen, the idea had a chance to spread, and, it seems to me, awakened interest all around" (see p. 3).

41. Münsterberg, "Why We Go to the Movies," 24. Münsterberg had at least on one occasion recorded a highly negative evaluation of the movies. In 1914 he wrote: "By what wholesome appeals to the desire for amusement can the masses be diverted from the unhealthy influence of the motion pictures which too often make crime and vice seductive and create a hysteric attitude by their thrills and horrors?" (see Hugo Münsterberg, *Psychology: General and Applied* (New York: D. Appleton & Co., 1925), 454. The volume was first published 1914.

42. Schweinitz, 13.

43. Ibid., 12.

44. For Münsterberg's contributions to psychology discussed in a more philosophical context see Bruce Kuklick's chapter on Münsterberg in *The Rise of American Philosophy*, 196–214, see note 13.

45. Noël Carroll, "Film/Mind Analogies: The Case of Hugo Münsterberg, *Journal of Aesthetics and Art Criticism* 46, n. 4 (Summer, 1988): 489–499.

46. Nyyssonen, "Film Theory at the Turning Point of Modernity," 1–2. See note 7 for full citation. Nyyssonen directs our attention to Joseph Anderson's *The Reality of Illusions: An Ecological Approach to Cognitive Film Theory* (Carbondale: Southern Illinois University Press, 1996); Murray Smith, *Engaging Characters/ Fiction, Emotion and Cinema* (London, New York, Oxford: Oxford University Press, 1995); Ed S. Tan, *Emotion and Structure of Narrative Film*, trans. by Barbara Fasting (Mawah, N.J.: Lawrence Erlbaum Associates, 1996). In addition to these might be added the special volume of the journal *IRIS*, volume 9 (Spring, 1989), and its follow-up volume (Summer, 1990); Torben Grodal's *Moving Pictures: A New Theory of Film Genres, Feelings, and Cognition* (New York: Oxford University Press, 1997); Edward Branigan's *Narrative Comprehension and Film* (London: Routledge, 1992); and Carl Plantinga & Greg M. Smith, eds., *Passionate Views: Film, Cognition, and Emotion* (Baltimore: The Johns Hopkins University Press, 1999). Warren Buckland's recent book *Cognitive Semiotics of Film* (Cambridge & New York: Cambridge University Press, 2000), attempts to referee the debate between a North American group of cognitivists (Bordwell, Carroll, Branigan, Anderson) who reject the semiotic tradition, and a group of European film theorists (Francesco Casetti, Roger Odin, Michael Colin, Dominique Chateau) who are trying to reconcile semiotic and cognitive film theories. A notable contribution in this vein is Martha E. Hensley's Master's thesis, *Hugo Münsterberg: Proto-cognitivist in the Classic Tradition*, University of Kansas, 1994. Even so, not all scholars interested in cognitive film theory are sympathetic to Münsterberg's ideas about film. See Gregory Currie, *Image and Mind: Film, philosophy and cognitive science* (New York: Cambridge University Press, 1995), xxiii.

47. For example, there are several relevant points of comparison between Münsterberg and Jean Epstein's film theory of the early 1920s; or even Victor O. Freeburg's work on film, for that matter. Malcolm Turvey's essay on Epstein, positioned within discourses on ocularcentrism and antiocularcentrism and examined through the lens of Wittgenstein's concept of "aspect dawning," gives us provocative cues as to the directions such a more sophisticated account of Münsterberg's ideas might take. Malcolm Turvey, "The Rehabilitation of the Corporeal Eye," *October* 83 (Winter, 1998): 25–50.

48. It is questionable whether Vachel Lindsay's *Art of the Moving Picture*, which came out the year before *The Photoplay*, can be classified as "theoretical," at least in the same sense. The jump from "early" to more "modern" theorizing is usually made from Münsterberg to Rudolf Arnheim's *Film as Art* of 1933, since many of Arnheim's ideas echo Münsterberg's: the unreality of the medium, the purity of the medium, the proscription against supplementing the image with sound and color, and even Arnheim's concept of "partial illusion" seems to parallel Münsterberg. Yet it is very unlikely that Arnheim had ever seen a copy of *The Photoplay*. More probably the similarities between Arnheim and Münsterberg stem from a common educational background in Germany where the two were exposed to similar Kantian philosophies of art and aesthetic attitudes. In terms of their psychology, Arnheim's Gestalt orientation originated in the anti-Wundtian psychologies instigated, in part, by Münsterberg himself during his years in Germany. However, Pasi Nyyssonen warns against categorizing Münsterberg with the Gestalt psychologists, or even considering him a proto-Gestalt figure, as Dudley Andrew and Jacques Aumont have done. Even though Münsterberg challenged Wundt on several points, Nyyssonen suggests that Münsterberg "remained in the Wundtian legacy of atomistic psychology." See Nyyssonen, 4–5 and Rudolf Arnheim, *Film as Art* (Berkeley: University of California Press, 1967). First published as *Film als Kunst* in 1933. The same is true of Kracauer, where Kracauer's discussion of film and live theater is comparable to Münsterberg, even if Kracauer's examination of the issue is far more sophisticated. Siegfried Kracauer, *Theory of Film. The Redemption of Physical Reality* (Princeton: Princeton University Press, 1997). This edition has an excellent introduction by Miriam Bratu Hansen.

49. Donald Laurence Fredericksen, *The Aesthetic of Isolation in Film Theory: Hugo Münsterberg* (New York: Arno Press, 1977). Fredericksen's book broke decades of relative silence over *The Photoplay* and it remains the most important analysis of Münsterberg's book. The volume was derived from Fredericksen's doctoral thesis at the University of Iowa in 1973. Other scholars have explored the relation between *The Photoplay* and notable films of the times, such as D. W. Griffith's *The Birth of a Nation*, which came out the very year that Münsterberg was watching films while researching *The Photoplay*. See Elaine Mancini, "Theory and Practice: Hugo Münsterberg and the Early films of D. W. Griffith," *New Orleans Review* 10, 2–3 (Summer-Fall, 1983): 154–160.

50. See a brief account in Hugo Münsterberg, "Psychology and the Market," *McClure's Magazine* 34, n. 1 (November, 1909): 87–93.

51. Phyllis Keller's *States of Belonging* is an exception.

52. I have provided full citations for these studies in the text of *The Photoplay*.

53. See Hugo Münsterberg, "Connection in Science and Isolation in Art," in *A Modern Book of Esthetics: An Anthology*, 3rd edition, edited by Melvin Rader (New York: Holt, Rinehart, & Winston Inc., 1960): 436. This piece was adapted from Münsterberg's *Principles of Art Education* of 1905. For a provocative account of some of Münsterberg's other views on science, art, and aesthetics see his "Psychology and Art," *Atlantic Monthly* 82, n. 493 (November, 1898): 632–643.

54. Münsterberg, "Connection in Science and Isolation in Art," 437.

55. Ibid. See also, Fredericksen, *The Aesthetic of Isolation in Film Theory: Hugo Münsterberg.* Münsterberg also gives an extensive discussion of aesthetic isolation in "The Problem of Beauty," *The Philosophical Review*, 18, n. 2 (March, 1909): 121–146. See especially pp. 135–7.

56. Münsterberg mentions here his own ventures in film making by promoting the *Paramount Pictographs*, the "magazine on the screen," as a "bold step" in the innovation of educational films. See the text of the interview reprinted in this volume and note 40.

57. Münsterberg writes: "Yet the power of the moving pictures to supplement the school room and the newspaper and the library by spreading information and knowledge is, after all, secondary to their general task, to bring entertainment and amusement to the masses." Dudley Andrew, in his section on Münsterberg in *The Major Film Theories: An Introduction* (London, Oxford, & New York: Oxford University Press, 1976), 14–26, suggests a three stage development in Münsterberg: "The history of film," Andrew writes of Münsterberg's introduction, "shows an ineluctable propulsion from (stage one) the toying with visual gadgetry to (stage two) the serving of important societal functions such as education and information, and finally, through its natural affinity for narrative, to its true domain, (stage three) the mind of man" (see p. 16).

58. Münsterberg's adoption of the term "photoplay" in his title was no doubt encouraged by the recent labeling of moving pictures as "photoplays" by some of the larger film companies who wished to promote the notion of the film as a "highbrow" art like the theater play: literally a "photo play." Taking a position that must have delighted the movie industry, Münsterberg's argument focuses throughout on how film is not equal to but in fact superior to the stage.

59. In a related account of the perception of distance see Münsterberg's "Perception of Distance," *The Journal of Philosophy, Psychology and Scientific Methods* 1, n. 23 (November 10, 1904): 617–623. In this essay, Münsterberg gives an account of the verant lens developed by Carl Zeiss through which a flat photograph can be viewed in three dimensions with monocular vision. The account brings up issues regarding the

illusion of reality of the photographic medium and the perceptual mechanisms of the perception of dimensionality.

60. Compare Noël Burch's comments on the spectator's ideal position in front of the screen in *Theory of Film Practice* (Princeton: Princeton University Press, 1981), 35.

61. Baudry identified the historical source of such perspectival constructions in the Albertian vanishing point perspective of fifteenth-century Italian painting. For Baudry the importance of such a perspectival regime was the creation of a particularly activated and psychologically centralized viewing subject, where the spectator's eye is located at an ideal point directly opposite to the vanishing point of the representation, resulting in a sense of omnipotence and a feeling that the represented world is created for the self. Thus the cinematic apparatus plays a powerful ideological role in propagating the transcendental subject central to Western philosophy. Similarly, although certainly with no psychoanalytic musing, Münsterberg also equates the spectator's eye with the camera lens. Though Münsterberg does not make this explicit, the spectator's identification is therefore with the invisible parts of the apparatus (camera, projector), allowing for a pervasive illusion of "reality" and omnipotence. See Jean-Louis Baudry, "Ideological Effects of the Basic Cinematic Apparatus," in *A Film Theory Reader. Narrative, Apparatus, Ideology*, edited by Philip Rosen (New York: Columbia University Press, 1986), 286–298; and in the same volume, Baudry's "The Apparatus: Metapsychological Approaches to the Impression of Reality in the Cinema," pp. 299–318.

62. Except perhaps in the case of "trick pictures," such as "Princess Nicotina," which Münsterberg mentions in passing in *The Photoplay*.

63. Also sometimes referred to as "The Shifted Checkerboard Illusion" or "The Münsterberg Café Wall Illusion." See P. Bressan, "Revisitation of the Family Tie between the Münsterberg and Taylor-Woodhouse Illusions," *Perception*, 14 (1985): 579–585; and R. H. Day, "A Note on the Münsterberg or Café Wall Illusion," *Perception* 7 (1978): 123–124. Münsterberg even collaborated with the Milton Bradley game company and published a collection of illusions in 1894 which they called "Pseudoptics."

64. See Hale, *Human Science*, pp. 35–37.

65. Hale, *Human Science*, 146. For Hale's account of Münsterberg's theory and its relation to British associationism, see pages 38–39.

66. Greater attention is given to these categories in the section on the fluctuations of attention in Hugo Münsterberg, *Beiträge zur experimentellen Psychologie*, (Freiburg: J. C. B. Mohr, 1889–92). However, Münsterberg elsewhere seems to see the distinction between voluntary and involuntary attention as being less important when considering the mind's response. Whether the stimulus comes from within or without, the mind still works upon the "object" of thought and attention in a similar way. See his discussion of the two concepts in Münsterberg, *Psychology: General and Applied*, 188. Contemporary psychology distinguishes between the broad categories of focal and automatic attention.

67. It is true that we may choose at some point to look at an actor whom we like even when he or she is not speaking, thus forcing our voluntary attention on the scene. However Münsterberg suggests that, "By such behavior we break the spell in which the artistic drama ought to hold us. We disregard the real shadings of the play and by mere personal side interests put emphasis where it does not belong. If we really enter into the spirit of the play, our attention is constantly drawn in accordance with the intentions of the producers."

68. S. M. Eisenstein, *Selected Works, vol. 1, Writings 1922–34*, trans. Richard Taylor (Bloomington: Indiana University Press, 1988). See "The Montage of Attractions," pp. 33–38, and "The Montage of Film Attractions," pp. 39–58.

69. Hugo Münsterberg, *Psychology and Industrial Efficiency* (Boston: Houghton Mifflin, 1913), 136.

70. Ibid., 136–137. While acuity of eyesight, reaction times, and other physiological factors are important, Münsterberg—in his consideration of the problem of creating psychological experiments to measure the aptitudes of potential electric trolley operators—saw attention as the primary factor: " . . . in the case of the motorman I abstracted from the study of single elementary functions and turned my attention to that mental process which after some careful observations seemed to me the really central one for the problem of accidents. I found this to be a particular complicated act of attention by which the manifoldness of objects, the pedestrians, the carriages, and the automobiles, are cont-inuously observed with reference to their rapidity and direction in the quickly changing panorama of the street." Ibid., 65–66. See also Münsterberg, *Psychology: General and Applied*, 129. For an example of experimental work directed by Münsterberg at his laboratory at Harvard see his student's publication: H. C. McComas, "Some Types of Attention," *The Psychological Monographs* 13, n. 3 (May, 1911): 1–55.

71. Münsterberg, *Psychology and Industrial Efficiency* , 135–136.

72. One of the subdivisions of Münsterberg's discussion of attention in the film is vividness. Vividness is the immediate mental result of attention whereby the object attended to is brought to the center of consciousness. In Münsterberg's concept of mental functions vividness is the first of four components that work in concert to construct a complete act of attention. The second component is inhibition, the marginalizing of other sensory stimulation which might compete with and thereby undermine the attention to the particular thing. Münsterberg describes this as a suppression of the objects not attended to (it is only these first two that he mentions in *The Photoplay*). The third element of attention is composed of both the mental and base physical actions which are generated by the perception. These include thoughts (should I run?!), feelings (fear), and bodily sensations (blushing, adrenaline rushes, sweating). The forth element which completes a full attentive act is the adjustment of the body to the stimulus, thus sending, as he puts it, "kinesthetic sensations to consciousness" (run!). As Münsterberg notes, "The content on which the attention

focuses thus becomes the center from which all the further psychophysical develop-ments irradiate." See Münsterberg, *Psychology: General and Applied*, 189–191. See also Münsterberg, *Psychology and Industrial Efficiency*, 261–263, where vividness is dis-cussed in terms of effective advertising.

73. Here too we find elements expressed in Münsterberg's other work. Memory, for example, is a central component of his consideration of the psychology of the wit-ness in his book *On the Witness Stand*, Münsterberg's early contribution to forensic psychology. Moreover, the best electric trolley operators, mentioned above, have a mental type which can unify various kinds of data, "which may be understood as a particular combination of attention and imagination." Such persons must be able to use their imaginations to predict whether someone or something *might* make a fatal move into the path of the trolley. See Münsterberg, *Psychology and Industrial Efficien-cy*, 66. Münsterberg's discussion of memory and imagination in *The Photoplay* are fairly simple, but he makes much finer distinctions between the two categories in *Psychology: General and Applied*, 165–175.

74. Münsterberg, *On the Witness Stand*, see especially the chapter "Suggestions in Court," pp. 175–199.

75. Münsterberg, *Psychology and Industrial Efficiency*, 273–5, and the chapter "Buying and Selling," pp. 294–302.

76. It was this early model Eisenstein was obliged to modify in his later career, for which he invented he concept of "inner speech" to give the viewer, theoretically, a role in the "free" play of associations in concert with the film narrative. Münsterberg never gives the spectator a creative role. Eisenstein's notion of "inner speech" is explained in his "Montage 1938" in S. M. Eisenstein, *Selected Works vol. II* (London: BFI, 1991): 296–311. For Eisenstein's modification of his model, see David Bordwell, "Eisenstein's Epistemological Shift," *Screen* 15, n. 4 (Winter 1974–5): 32–46. Note Ben Brewster's preliminary comments pp. 29–32, and Bordwell's response on pp. 142–3.

77. Münsterberg waxes Albertian when discussing this empathetic aspect of the new art: "We sympathize with the sufferer . . . We share the joy of the happy lover and the grief of the despondent mourner, we feel the indignation of the betrayed wife and the fear of the man in danger." Compare Leon Battista Alberti's comments from *On Painting*: "The istoria will move the soul of the beholder when each man painted there clearly shows the movements of his own soul. It happens in nature that nothing more than herself is found capable of things like herself; we weep with the weeping, laugh with the laughing, and grieve with the grieving. These movements of the soul are made known by the movements of the body." See Leon Battista Alberti, *On Painting*, trans. John R. Spencer (New Haven & London: Yale University Press, 1966): 77.

78. We are very much reminded of Rudolf Arnheim and his concept of "partial illusion" as outlined in the "Film and Reality" section of *Film as Art*, pp. 8–34.

79. Münsterberg's theory on the social functions of art and film are not all that different from his theories on the function of alcohol. In his article "Prohibition

and Social Psychology," *McClure's Magazine* 31, n. 4 (August, 1908): 438–444, Münsterberg notes that having a beer or two at the end of the day gives the working masses a reprieve from their labors which is both physiological and psychological. He writes on page 443: "The American masses work hard throughout the day. The sharp physical and mental labor, the constant hurry and drudgery produce a state of tension and irritation which demands before the night's sleep some dulling inhibition if a dangerous unrest is not to set in. Alcohol relieves that daily tension most directly." The key term in the passage is "inhibition," a concept central to many of Münsterberg's work in psychology. It is a mild repression which is often part of healthy mental life. For Münsterberg, film, like any art form that encourages contemplation in "aesthetic isolation," clearly inhibits ones connection with the stress and strain of every day reality and the "real" outer world.

80. One could certainly argue with Münsterberg's claims about the limitations of stagecraft, and scholars criticizing Münsterberg—from the initial critical reception to more contemporary accounts—have taken the opportunity to defend the theater from his constraining definitions. The first such objection came from an unidentified reviewer in *The Dramatist* (July, 1916): 714–15. A more sustained critique is Mark Wicclair, "Film Theory and Hugo Münsterberg's *The Film A Psychological Study*," *The Journal of Aesthetic Education* 12, n. 3 (July, 1978): 33–50.

81. A more sustained reflection on this very aspect of film, and one which Münsterberg would no doubt have agreed with, can be found in Rudolf Arnheim's 1938 essay "A New Laocoön: Artistic Composites and the Talking Film" in *Film as Art*, 199–230.

82. Münsterberg, *Psychology and Industrial Efficiency*, 206–220.

83. The issue of the use of color is also touched upon. Even though Münsterberg is willing to admit some positive expressive and descriptive potentials in the use of coloration, it, like speech, is a supplement which transgresses the boundaries of film art. Color brings the film too close to reality, threatening to make it as garish and banal as the figure in a wax museum. "We do not want to paint the cheeks of the Venus of Milo," he writes, and "neither do we want to see the coloring of Mary Pickford or Anita Stewart." As we move towards exact mimesis of the real world, we lose that very freedom and isolation that facilitates the aesthetic experience of the work of art. Here we find Rudolf Arnheim in accord with Münsterberg. For Arnheim too, color brought the film image closer to reality, thereby undermining that part of the medium which could be used for expressive, artistic ends.

84. A purview of the usages in film magazines contemporary with *The Photoplay*, such as the *New York Dramatic Mirror* and *Moving Picture World*, reveal an alternation of the two terms director and producer, indicating that they were often used interchangeably.

85. Münsterberg does not address the issue of the relative artistic merits of the

cinematographer and editor. Probably he would see these two individuals as simply obeying the artistic guidelines set by the producer/director.

86. Münsterberg seems to be a strong supporter of self-censorship in this arena, lauding "leading" film companies that "fight everywhere in the first rank for the suppression of the unclean." And he furthermore notes, in accord with contemporary debates on the issue, that government censorship may not be "in harmony with American ideas on the freedom of pubic expression." Münsterberg may be challenging the National Board of Censorship, founded in 1909 and funded by the Motion Picture Patents Trust (renamed the National Board of Review in 1916, the year *The Photoplay* was published).

87. Hale, *Human Science*, 147.

88. I am referring to Walter Benjamin's, "The Work of Art in the Age of Mechanical Reproduction" of 1935. See Walter Benjamin, *Illuminations*, edited by Hannah Arendt and translated by Henry Zohn (New York: Harcourt, Brace, World, 1968).

The Photoplay:
A Psychological Study

Introduction

Chapter 1: The Outer Development of the Moving Pictures

It is arbitrary to say where the development of the moving pictures began and it is impossible to foresee where it will lead. What invention marked the beginning? Was it the first device to introduce movement into the pictures on a screen? Or did the development begin with the first photographing of various phases of moving objects? Or did it start with the first presentation of successive pictures at such a speed that the impression of movement resulted? Or was the birthday of the new art when the experimenters for the first time succeeded in projecting such rapidly passing pictures on a wall? If we think of the moving pictures as a source of entertainment and aesthetic enjoyment, we may see the germ in that camera obscura which allowed one glass slide to pass before another and thus showed the railway train on one slide moving over the bridge on the other glass plate. They were popular half a century ago. On the other hand if the essential feature of the moving pictures is the combination of various views into one connected impression, we must look back to the days of the phenakistoscope which had scientific interest only; it is more than eighty years since it was invented. In America, which in most recent times has become the classical land of the moving picture production, the history may be said to begin with the days of the Chicago Exposition, 1893, when Edison exhibited his kinetoscope. The visitor dropped his nickel into a slot, the little motor started, and for half a minute he saw through the magnifying glass a girl dancing or some street boys fighting. Less than a quarter of a century later twenty thousand theaters for moving pictures are open daily in the United States and the millions get for their nickel long hours of enjoyment. In Edison's small box into which only one at a time could peep through the hole, nothing but a few trite scenes were exhibited. In those twenty thousand theaters which grew from it, all human passions and emotions find their stage, and whatever history reports or science demonstrates or imagination invents comes to life on the screen of the picture palace.

Yet this development from Edison's half-minute show to *The Birth of a Nation* did not proceed on American soil. That slot box, after all, had little chance for popular success. The decisive step was taken when pictures of the Edison type were for the first time thrown on a screen and thus made visible to a large audience. That step was taken in 1895 in London. The moving picture theater certainly began in England. But there was one source of the stream springing up in America, which long preceded Edison: the photographic efforts of the Englishman Muybridge, who made his experiments in California as early as 1872. His aim was to have photographs of various phases of a continuous movement, for instance of the different positions which a trotting horse is passing through. His purpose was the analysis of the movement into its component parts, not the synthesis of a moving picture from such parts. Yet it is evident that this too was a necessary step which made the later triumphs possible.

If we combine the scientific and the artistic efforts of the new and the old world, we may tell the history of the moving pictures by the following dates and achievements. In the year 1825, a Doctor Roget described in the *Philosophical Transactions* an interesting optical illusion of movement, resulting, for instance, when a wheel is moving along behind a fence of upright bars.[1] The discussion was carried much further when it was taken up a few years later by a master of the craft, by Faraday. In the *Journal of the Royal Institute of Great Britain* he writes in 1831 "on a peculiar class of optical deceptions."[2] He describes there a large number of subtle experiments in which cogwheels of different forms and sizes were revolving with different degrees of rapidity and in different directions. The eye saw the cogs of the moving rear wheel through the passing cogs of the front wheel. The result is the appearance of movement effects which do not correspond to an objective motion. The impression of backward movement can arise from forward motions, quick movement from slow, complete rest from combinations of movements. For the first time the impression of movement was synthetically produced from different elements. For those who fancy that the "new psychology" with its experimental analysis of psychological experiences began only in the second half of the nineteenth century or perhaps even with the foundation of the psychological laboratories, it might be enlightening to study those discussions of the early thirties.

The next step leads us much further. In the fall of 1832, Stampfer in Germany and Plateau in France, independent of each other, at the same time designed a device by which pictures of objects in various phases of movement give the impression of continued motion.[3] Both secured the effect by cutting fine slits in a black disk in the direction of the radius. When the disk is revolved around its center, these slits pass the eye of the observer. If he holds it before a mirror and on the rear side of the disk pictures are drawn corresponding to the various slits, the eye will see one picture after another in rapid succession at the same place. If these little pictures give us the various stages of a movement, for instance a wheel with its spokes in different positions, the whole series of impressions will be combined into the perception of a revolving wheel. Stampfer called them the stroboscopic disks, Plateau the phenakistoscope. The smaller the slits, the sharper the pictures. Uchatius in Vienna constructed an apparatus as early as 1853 to throw these pictures of the stroboscopic disks on the wall.[4] Horner followed with the daedaleum, in which the disk was replaced by a hollow cylinder which had the pictures on the inside and holes to watch them from without while the cylinder was in rotation.[5] From this was developed the popular toy which as the zoötrope or bioscope became familiar everywhere. It was a revolving black cylinder with vertical slits, on the inside of which paper strips with pictures of moving objects in successive phases were placed. The clowns sprang through the hoop and repeated this whole movement with every new revolution of the cylinder. In more complex instruments, three sets of slits were arranged above one another. One set corresponded exactly to the distances of the pictures and the result was that the moving object appeared to remain on the same spot. The second brought the slits nearer together; then the pictures necessarily produced an effect as if the man were really moving forward while he performed his tricks. In the third set the slits were further distant from one another than the pictures, and the result was that the picture moved backward.

The scientific principle which controls the moving picture world of today was established with these early devices. Isolated pictures, presented to the eye in rapid succession but separated by interruptions, are perceived not as single impressions of different positions, but as a continuous movement. But the pictures of movements used so far were drawn by the pen of the artist. Life showed to him everywhere continuous movements; his imagination had to resolve them into various instantaneous positions. He drew the horse race for the zoötrope, but while the horses moved forward, nobody was able to say whether the various pictures of their legs really corresponded to the stages of the actual movements. Thus a true development of the stroboscopic effects appeared dependent upon the fixation of the successive stages. This was secured in the early seventies, but to make this progress possible, the whole wonderful unfolding of the photographer's art was needed, from the early daguerreotype, which presupposed hours of exposure, to the instantaneous photograph which fixes the picture of the outer world in a small fraction of a second. We are not concerned here with this technical advance, with the perfection of the sensitive surface of the photographic plate. In 1872, the photographer's camera had reached a stage at which it was possible to take snapshot pictures. But this alone would not have allowed the photographing of a real movement with one camera, as the plates could not have been exchanged quickly enough to catch the various phases of a short motion.

Here the work of Muybridge sets in. He had a black horse trot or gallop or walk before a white wall, passing twenty-four cameras. On the path of the horse were twenty-four threads which the horse broke one after another and each one released the spring which opened the shutter of an instrument. The movement of the horse was thus analyzed into twenty-four pictures of successive phases; and for the first time the human eye saw the actual positions of a horse's legs during the gallop or trot. It is not surprising that these pictures of Muybridge interested the French painters when he came to Paris, but fascinated still more the great student of animal movements, the physiologist Marey.[6] He had contributed to science many an intricate apparatus for the registration of movement processes. "Marey's tambour" is still the most useful instrument in every physiological and psychological laboratory, whenever slight delicate movements are to be recorded. The movement of a bird's wings interested him especially, and at his suggestion Muybridge turned to the study of the flight of birds. Flying pigeons were photographed in different positions, each picture taken in a five-hundredth part of a second.

But Marey himself improved the method. He made use of an idea which the astronomer Janssen had applied to the photographing of astronomical processes.[7] Janssen photographed, for instance, the transit of the planet Venus across the sun in December, 1874, on a circular sensitized plate which revolved in the camera. The plate moved forward a few degrees every minute. There was room in this way to have eighteen pictures of different phases of the transit on the marginal part of the one plate. Marey constructed the apparatus for the revolving disk so that the intervals instead of a full minute became only one-twelfth of a second. On the one revolving disk twenty-five views of the bird in motion could be taken. This brings us to the time of the early eighties. Marey remained indefatigable in improving the means for quick successive snapshots with the same camera. Human beings were photographed by him in white clothes on a black background. When ten pictures were taken in a second the subtlest motions in their jumping or running could be disentangled. The leading aim was still decidedly a scientific understanding of the motions, and the combination of the pictures into a unified impression of movement was not the purpose. Least of all was mere amusement intended.

About that time, Anschütz in Germany followed the Muybridge suggestions with much success and gave to this art of photographing the movement of animals and men a new turn.[8] He not only photographed the successive stages, but printed them on a long strip which was laid around a horizontal wheel. This wheel is in a dark box and the eye can see the pictures on the paper strip only at the moment when the light of a Geissler's tube flashes up. The wheel itself has such electric contacts that the intervals between two flashes correspond to the time that is necessary to move the wheel from one picture to the next. However quickly the wheel may be revolved the lights follow one another with the same rapidity with which the pictures replace one another. During the movement when one picture moves away and another approaches the center of vision all is dark. Hence, the eye does not see the changes but gets an impression as if the picture remained at the same spot, only moving. The bird flaps its wings and the horse trots. It was really a perfect kinetoscopic instrument. Yet its limitations were evident. No movements could be presented but simple rhythmical ones, inasmuch as after one revolution of the wheel the old pictures returned. The marching men appeared very lifelike; yet they could not do anything but march on and on, the circumference of the wheel not allowing more room than was needed for about forty stages of the moving legs from the beginning to the end of the step.

If the picture of a motion was to go beyond these simplest rhythmical movements, if persons in action were really to be shown, it would be necessary to have a much larger number of pictures in instantaneous illumination. The wheel principle would have to be given up and a long strip with pictures would be needed. That presupposed a correspondingly long set of exposures and this demand could not be realized as long as the pictures were taken on glass plates. But, in that period, experiments were undertaken on many sides to substitute a more flexible transparent material for the glass. Translucent papers, gelatine, celluloid, and other substances were tried. It is well known that the invention which was decisive was the film which Eastman in Rochester produced. With it came the great mechanical improvement, the use of the two rollers. One roller holds the long strip of film which is slowly wound over the second, the device familiar to every amateur photographer today. With film photography was gained the possibility, not only of securing a much larger number of pictures than Marey or Anschütz made with their circular arrangements, but of having these pictures pass before the eye illumined by quickly succeeding flashlights for any length of time. Moreover, instead of the quick illumination, the passing pictures might be constantly lighted. In that case slits must pass by in the opposite direction so that each picture is seen for a moment only, as if it were at rest. This idea is perfectly realized in Edison's machine.

In Edison's kinetoscope, a strip of celluloid film forty-five feet in length with a series of pictures each three-quarters of an inch long moved continuously over a series of rolls. The pictures passed a magnifying lens, but between the lens and the picture was a revolving shutter which moved with a speed carefully adjusted to the film. The opening in the shutter was opposite the lens at the moment when the film had moved on three-quarters of an inch. Hence, the eye saw not the passing of the pictures but one picture after another at the same spot. Pretty little scenes could now be acted in half a minute's time, as more than six hundred pictures could be used. The first instrument was built in 1890, and soon after the Chicago World's Fair it was used for entertainment all over the world. The wheel of Anschütz had been widespread too; yet it was considered only as a half-scientific apparatus. With Edison's kinetoscope, the moving pictures had become a means for popular amusement and entertainment, and the appetite of commercialism was whetted. At once, efforts to improve on the Edison machine were starting everywhere, and the adjustment to the needs of the wide public was in the foreground.

Crowning success came almost at the same time to Lumière and Son in Paris and to Paul in London.[9] They recognized clearly that the new scheme could not become really profitable on a large scale as long as only one person at a time could see the pictures. Both the well-known French manufacturers of photographic supplies and the English engineer considered the next step necessary to be the projection of the films upon a large screen. Yet this involved another fundamental change. In the kinetoscope, the films passed by continuously. The time of the exposure through the opening in the revolving shutter had to be extremely short in order to give distinct pictures. The slightest lengthening would make the movement of the film itself visible and produce a blurring effect. This time was sufficient for the seeing of the picture; it could not be sufficient for the greatly enlarged view on the wall. Too little light passed through to give a distinct image. Hence it became essential to transform the continuous movement of the film into an intermittent one. The strip of film must be drawn before the lens by jerking movements so that the real motion of the strip would occur in the periods in which the shutter was closed, while it was at rest for the fraction of time in which the light of the projection apparatus passed through.

Both Lumière and Paul overcame this difficulty and secured an intermittent pushing forward of the pictures for three-quarters of an inch, that is for the length of the single photograph. In the spring of 1895, Paul's theatrograph or animatograph was completed; and in the following year, he began his engagement at the Alhambra Theater, where the novelty was planned as a vaudeville show for a few days but stayed for many a year, since it proved at once an unprecedented success. The American field was conquered by the Lumière camera. The Eden Musée was the first place where this French kinematograph was installed. The enjoyment which today one hundred and twenty-five thousand moving picture theaters all over the globe bring to thirty million people daily is dependent upon Lumière's and Paul's invention. The improvements in the technique of taking the pictures and of projecting them on the screen are legion, but the fundamental features have not been changed. Yes; on the whole the development of the last two decades has been a conservative one. The fact that every producer tries to distribute his films to every country forces a far-reaching standardization on the entire moving picture world. The little pictures on the film are still today exactly the same size as those which Edison used for his kinetoscope and the long strips of film are still gauged by four round perforations at the side of each to catch the sprockets which guide the film.

As soon as the moving picture show had become a feature of the vaudeville theater, the longing of the crowd for ever new entertainments and sensations had to be satisfied if the success was to last. The mere enjoyment of the technical wonder as such necessarily faded away, and the interest could be kept up only if the scenes presented on the screen became themselves more and more enthralling. The trivial acts played in less than a minute without any artistic setting and without any rehearsal or preparation soon became unsatisfactory. The grandmother who washes the baby and even the street boy who plays a prank had to be replaced by quick little comedies. Stages were set up; more and more elaborate scenes were created; the film grew and grew in length. Competing companies in France and later in the United States, England, Germany, and notably in Italy developed more and more ambitious productions. As early as 1898, the Eden Musée in New York produced an elaborate setting of the Passion Play in nearly fifty thousand pictures, which needed almost an hour for production. The personnel on the stage increased rapidly, huge establishments in which any scenery could be built up sprang into being. But the enclosed scene was often not a sufficient background; the kinematographic camera was brought to mountains and seashore, and soon to the jungles of Africa or to Central Asia if the photoplay demanded exciting scenes or picturesque backgrounds. Thousands of people entered into the battle scenes which the historical drama demanded. We stand today in the midst of this external growth of which no one dreamed in the days of the kinetoscope. Yet this technical progress and this tremendous increase of the mechanical devices for production have their true meaning in the inner growth which led from trite episodes to the height of tremendous action, from trivial routine to a new and most promising art.

Chapter 2: The Inner Development of the Moving Pictures

It was indeed not an external technical advance only which led from Edison's half a minute show of the little boy who turns on the hose to *The Daughter of Neptune* [*Neptune's Daughter* (Ed.)], or *Quo Vadis*, or *Cabiria*, and many another performance which fills an evening. The advance was first of all internal; it was an aesthetic idea. Yet even this does not tell the whole story of the inner growth of the moving pictures, as it points only to the progress of the photoplay. It leaves out of account the fact that the moving pictures appeal not merely to the imagination, but that they bring their message also to the intellect. They aim toward instruction and information. Just as, between the two covers of a magazine, artistic stories stand side by side with instructive essays, scientific articles, or discussions of the events of the day, the photoplay is accompanied by a kinematoscopic rendering of reality in all its aspects. Whatever in nature or in social life interests the human understanding or human curiosity comes to the mind of the spectator with an incomparable intensity when not a lifeless photograph but a moving picture brings it to the screen.

The happenings of the day afford the most convenient material, as they offer the chance for constantly changing programmes and hence the ideal conditions for a novelty-seeking public. No actors are needed; the dramatic interest is furnished by the political and social importance of the events. In the early days, when the great stages for the production of photoplays had not been built, the moving picture industry relied in a much higher degree than today on this supply from the surrounding public life. But while the material was abundant, it soon became rather insipid to see parades and processions and orators, and even where the immediate interest seemed to give value to the pictures it was for the most part only a local interest and faded away after a time. The coronation of the king or the inauguration of the president, the earthquake in Sicily, the great Derby, come, after all, too seldom. Moreover through the strong competition only the first comer gained the profits and only the most sensational dashes of kinematographers with the reporter's instinct could lead to success in the eyes of the spoiled moving picture audiences.

Certainly the history of these enterprises is full of adventures worthy to rank with the most daring feats in the newspaper world. We hear that when the investiture of the Prince of Wales was performed at Carnarvon at four o'clock in the afternoon, the public of London at ten o'clock of the same day saw the ceremony on the screen in a moving picture twelve minutes in length. The distance between the two places is two hundred miles. The film was seven hundred and fifty feet long. It had been developed and printed in a special express train made up of long freight cars transformed into dark rooms and fitted with tanks for the developing and washing and with a machine for printing and drying. Yet on the whole, the current events were slowly losing ground even in Europe, while America had never given such a large share of interest to this rival of the newspaper. It is claimed that the producers in America disliked these topical pictures because the accidental character of the events makes the production irregular and interferes too much with the steady preparation of the photoplays. Only when the war broke out, the great wave of excitement swept away this apathy. The pictures from the trenches, the marches of the troops, the life of the prisoners, the movements of the leaders, the busy life behind the front, and the action of the big guns absorbed the popular interest in every corner of the world. While the picturesque old-time war reporter has almost disappeared, the moving picture man has inherited all his courage, patience, sensationalism, and spirit of adventure.

A greater photographic achievement, however, than the picturing of the social and historic events was the marvelous success of the kinematograph with the life of nature. No explorer in recent years has crossed distant lands and seas without a kinematographic outfit. We suddenly looked into the most intimate life of the African wilderness. There, the elephants and giraffes and monkeys passed to the water-hole, not knowing that the moving picture man was turning his crank in the top of a tree. We followed Scott and Shackleton into the regions of eternal ice, we climbed the Himalayas, we saw the world from the height of the aeroplane, and every child in Europe knows now the wonders of Niagara. But the kinematographer has not sought nature only where it is gigantic or strange; he follows its path with no less admirable effect when it is idyllic. The brook in the woods, the birds in their nest, the flowers trembling in the wind have brought their charm to the delighted eye more and more with the progress of the new art.

But the wonders of nature which the camera unveils to us are not limited to those which the naked eye can follow. The technical progress led to the attachment of the microscope. After overcoming tremendous difficulties, the scientists succeeded in developing a microscope kinematography which multiplies the dimensions a hundred thousand times. We may see on the screen the fight of the bacteria with the microscopically small blood corpuscles in the blood stream of a diseased animal. Yes, by the miracles of the camera, we may trace the life of nature even in forms which no human observation really finds in the outer world. Out there, it may take weeks for the orchid to bud and blossom and fade; in the picture, the process passes before us in a few seconds. We see how the caterpillar spins its cocoon and how it breaks it and how the butterfly unfolds its wings; and all which needed days and months goes on in a fraction of a minute. New interest for geography and botany and zoology has thus been aroused by these developments, undreamed of in the early days of the kinematograph, and the scientists themselves have, through this new means of technique, gained unexpected help for their labors.

The last achievement in this universe of photoknowledge is "the magazine on the screen." It is a bold step which yet seemed necessary in our day of rapid kinematoscopic progress. The popular printed magazines in America had their heyday in the muckraking period about ten years ago. Their hold on the imagination of the public which wants to be informed and entertained at the same time has steadily decreased, while the power of the moving picture houses has increased. The picture house ought, therefore, to take up the task of the magazines which it has partly displaced. The magazines give only a small place to the news of the day, a larger place to articles in which scholars and men of public life discuss significant problems. Much American history in the last two decades was deeply influenced by the columns of the illustrated magazines. Those men who reached the millions by such articles cannot overlook the fact—they may approve or condemn it— that the masses of today prefer to be taught by pictures rather than by words. The audiences are assembled anyhow. Instead of feeding them with mere entertainment, why not give them food for serious thought? It seemed, therefore, a most fertile idea when the *Paramount Pictograph* was founded to carry intellectual messages and ambitious discussions into the film houses. Political and economic, social and hygienic, technical and industrial, aesthetic and scientific questions can in no way be brought nearer to the grasp of millions. The editors will have to take care that the discussions do not degenerate into one-sided propaganda, but so must the editors of a printed magazine. Among the scientists the psychologist may have a particular interest in this latest venture of the film world. The screen ought to offer a unique opportunity to interest wide circles in psychological experiments and mental tests and in this way to spread the knowledge of their importance for vocational guidance and the practical affairs of life.

Yet that power of the moving pictures to supplement the school room and the newspaper and the library by spreading information and knowledge is, after all, secondary to their general task, to bring entertainment and amusement to the masses. This is the chief road on which the forward march of the last twenty years has been most rapid. The theater and the vaudeville and the novel had to yield room and ample room to the play of the flitting pictures. What was the real principle of the inner development on this artistic side? The little scenes which the first pictures offered could hardly have been called plays. They would have been unable to hold the attention by their own contents. Their only charm was really the pleasure in the perfection with which the apparatus rendered the actual movements. But soon, touching episodes were staged, little humorous scenes or melodramatic actions were played before the camera, and the same emotions stirred which up to that time only the true theater play had awakened. The aim seemed to be to have a real substitute for the stage. The most evident gain of this new scheme was the reduction of expenses. One actor is now able to entertain many thousand audiences at the same time, one stage setting is sufficient to give pleasure to millions. The theater can thus be democratized. Everybody's purse allows him to see the greatest artists and in every village a stage can be set up, and the joy of a true theater performance can be spread to the remotest corner of the lands. Just as the graphophone can multiply without limit the music of the concert hall, the singer, and the orchestra, so, it seemed, would the photoplay reproduce the theater performance without end.

Of course, the substitute could not be equal to the original. The color was lacking, the real depth of the objective stage was missing, and above all the spoken word had been silenced. The few interspersed descriptive texts, the so-called leaders, had to hint at that which in the real drama the speeches of the actors explain and elaborate. It was thus surely only the shadow of a true theater, different not only as a photograph is compared with a painting, but different as a photograph is compared with the original man. And yet, however meager and shadowlike the moving picture play appeared compared with the performance of living actors, the advantage of the cheap multiplication was so great that the ambition of the producers was natural, to go forward from the little playlets to great dramas which held the attention for hours. The kinematographic theater soon had its Shakespeare repertoire; Ibsen has been played, and the dramatized novels on the screen became legion. Victor Hugo and Dickens scored new triumphs. In a few years, the way from the silly trite practical joke to *Hamlet* and *Peer Gynt* was covered with such thoroughness that the possibility of giving a photographic rendering of any think-able theater performance was proven for all time.

But while this movement to reproduce stage performances went on, elements were superadded, which the technique of the camera allowed, but which would hardly be possible in a theater. Hence the development led slowly to a certain deviation from the path of the drama. The difference which strikes the observer first results from the chance of the camera man to set his scene in the real background of nature and culture. The stage manager of the theater can paint the ocean and, if need be, can move some colored cloth to look like rolling waves; and yet how far is his effect surpassed by the superb ocean pictures when the scene is played on the real cliffs, and the waves are thundering at their foot, and the surf is foaming about the actors. The theater has its painted villages and vistas, its city streets and its foreign landscape backgrounds. But here the theater, in spite of the reality of the actors, appears thoroughly unreal compared with the throbbing life of the street scenes and of the foreign crowds in which the cameraman finds his local color.

But still more characteristic is the rapidity with which the whole background can be changed in the moving pictures. Reinhardt's re-volving stage had brought wonderful surprises to the theater-goer and had shifted the scene with a quickness which was unknown before. Yet how slow and clumsy does it remain compared with the routine changes of the photoplays. This changing of background is so easy for the camera that, at a very early date, this new feature of the plays was introduced. At first, it served mostly humorous purposes. The public of the crude early shows enjoyed the flashlike quickness with which it could follow the eloper over the roofs of the town, upstairs and down, into cellar and attic, and jump into the auto and race over the country roads until the culprit fell over a bridge into the water and was caught by the police. This slapstick humor has by no means dis-appeared, but the rapid change of scenes has meanwhile been put into the service of much higher aims. The development of an artistic plot has been brought to possibilities which the real drama does not know, by allowing the eye to follow the hero and heroine continuously from place to place. Now he leaves his room, now we see him passing along the street, now he enters the house of his beloved, now he is led into the parlor, now she is hurrying to the library of her father, now they all go to the garden: ever new stage settings sliding into one another. Technical difficulties do not stand in the way. A set of pictures taken by the camera man a thousand miles away can be inserted for a few feet in the film, and the audience sees now the clubroom in New York, and now the snows of Alaska, and now the tropics, near each other in the same reel.

Moreover, the ease with which the scenes are altered allows us not only to hurry on to ever new spots, but to be at the same time in two or three places. The scenes become intertwined. We see the soldier on the battlefield, and his beloved one at home, in such steady alternation that we are simultaneously here and there. We see the man speaking into the telephone in New York and at the same time the woman who receives his message in Washington. It is no difficulty at all for the photoplay to have the two alternate a score of times in the few minutes of the long distance conversation.

But with the quick change of background the photoartists also gained a rapidity of motion which leaves actual men behind. He needs only to turn the crank of the apparatus more quickly and the whole rhythm of the performance can be brought to a speed which may strikingly aid the farcical humor of the scene. And from here it was only a step to the performance of actions which could not be carried out in nature at all. At first this idea was made serviceable to rather rough comic effects. The policeman climbed up the solid stone front of a high building. The cameraman had no difficulty in securing the effects, as it was only necessary to have the actor creep over a flat picture of the building spread on the floor. Every day brought us new tricks. We see how the magician breaks one egg after another and takes out of each egg a little fairy and puts one after, another on his hand where they begin to dance a minuet. No theater could ever try to match such wonders, but for the camera they are not difficult; the little dancers were simply at a much further distance from the camera and, therefore, appeared in their Lilliputian size. Rich artistic effects have been secured, and, while on the stage every fairy play is clumsy and hardly able to create an illusion, in the film we really see the man transformed into a beast and the flower into a girl. There is no limit to the trick pictures which the skill of the experts invent. The divers jump, feet first, out of the water to the springboard. It looks magical, and yet the cameraman has simply to reverse his film and to run it from the end to the beginning of the action. Every dream becomes real, uncanny ghosts appear from nothing and disappear into nothing, mermaids swim through the waves, and little elves climb out of the Easter lilies.

As the crank of the camera which takes the pictures can be stopped at any moment and the turning renewed only after some complete change has been made on the stage any substitution can be carried out without the public knowing of the break in the events. We see a man walking to the edge of a steep rock, leaving no doubt that it is a real person, and then by a slip he is hurled down into the abyss below. The film does not indicate that, at the instant before the fall, the camera has been stopped and the actor replaced by a stuffed dummy, which begins to tumble when the movement of the film is started again. But not only dummies of the same size can be introduced. A little model brought quite near to the camera may take the place of the large real object at a far distance. We see at first the real big ship and can convince ourselves of its reality by seeing actual men climbing up the rigging. But when it comes to the final shipwreck, the movement of the film is stopped and the camera brought near to a little tank where a miniature model of the ship takes up the role of the original and explodes and really sinks to its two-feet-deep watery grave.

While, through this power to make impossible actions possible, unheard of effects could be reached, all still remained in the outer framework of the stage. The photoplay showed a performance, however rapid or unusual, as it would go on in the outer world. An entirely new perspective was opened when the managers of the film play introduced the close-up and similar new methods. As every friend of the film knows, the close-up is a scheme by which a particular part of the picture, perhaps only the face of the hero or his hand or only a ring on his finger, is greatly enlarged and replaces for an instant the whole stage. Even the most wonderful creations, the great historical plays where thousands fill the battlefields or the most fantastic caprices where fairies fly over the stage, could perhaps be performed in a theater, but this close-up leaves all stagecraft behind. Suddenly we see not Booth himself as he seeks to assassinate the president, but only his hand holding the revolver and the play of his excited fingers filling the whole field of vision. We no longer see at his desk the banker who opens the telegram, but the opened telegraphic message itself takes his place on the screen for a few seconds, and we read it over his shoulder.

It is not necessary to enumerate still more changes that the development of the art of the film has brought since the days of the kinetoscope. The use of natural backgrounds, the rapid change of scenes, the intertwining of the actions in different scenes, the changes of the rhythms of action, the passing through physically impossible experiences, the linking of disconnected movements, the realization of supernatural effects, the gigantic enlargement of small details: these may be sufficient as characteristic illustrations of the essential trend. They show that the progress of the photoplay did not lead to a more and more perfect photographic reproduction of the theater stage, but led away from the theater altogether. Superficial impressions suggest the opposite and still leave the aesthetically careless observer in the belief that the photoplay is a cheap substitute for the real drama, a theater performance as good or as bad as a photographic reproduction allows. But this traditional idea has become utterly untrue. *The art of the photoplay has developed so many new features of its own, features which have not even any similarity to the technique of the stage that the question arises: is it not really a new art which long since left behind the mere film reproduction of the theater and which ought to be acknowledged in its own aesthetic independence?* This right to independent recognition has so far been ignored. Practically everybody who judged the photoplays from the aesthetic point of view remained at the old comparison between the film and the graphophone. The photoplay is still something which simply imitates the true art of the drama on the stage. May it not be, on the contrary, that it does not imitate or replace anything, but is in itself an art as different from that of the theater as the painter's art is different from that of the sculptor? And may it not be high time, in the interest of theory and of practice, to examine the aesthetic conditions which would give independent rights to the new art? If this is really the situation, it must be a truly fascinating problem, as it would give the chance to watch the art in its first unfolding. A new aesthetic cocoon is broken; where will the butterfly's wings carry him?

We have at last reached the real problem of this little book. We want to study the right of the photoplay, hitherto ignored by aesthetics, to be classed as an art in itself under entirely new mental life conditions. What we need for this study is evidently, first, an insight into the means by which the moving pictures impress us and appeal to us. Not the physical means and technical devices are in question, but the mental means. What psychological factors are involved when we watch the happenings on the screen? But secondly, we must ask what characterizes the independence of an art, what constitutes the conditions under which the works of a special art stand. The first inquiry is psychological, the second aesthetic; the two belong intimately together. Hence we turn first to the psychological aspect of the moving pictures and later to the artistic one.

Part I: The Psychology of the Photoplay

Chapter 3: **Depth and Movement**

The problem is now quite clear before us. Do the photoplays furnish us only a photographic reproduction of a stage performance; is their aim, thus, simply to be an inexpensive substitute for the real theater, and is their aesthetic standing, accordingly, far below that of the true dramatic art, related to it as the photograph of a painting to the original canvas of the master? Or do the moving pictures bring us an independent art, controlled by aesthetic laws of its own, working with mental appeals which are fundamentally different from those of the theater, with a sphere of its own and with ideal aims of its own ? If this so far neglected problem is ours, we evidently need not ask in our further discussions about all which books on moving pictures have so far put into the foreground, namely the physical technique of producing the pictures on the film or of projecting the pictures on the screen, or anything else which belongs to the technical or physical or economic aspect of the photoplay industry. Moreover, it is then evidently not our concern to deal with those moving pictures which serve mere curiosity or the higher desires for information and instruction. Those educational pictures may give us delight, and certainly much aesthetic enjoyment may be combined with the intellectual satisfaction, when the wonders of distant lands are unveiled to us. The landscape setting of such a travel film may be a thing of beauty, but the pictures are not taken for art's sake: the aim is to serve the spread of knowledge.

Readers who have no technical interest in physiological psychology may omit Chapter 3 and turn directly to Chapter 4 on Attention [Münsterberg's note].

Our aesthetic interest turns to the means by which the photoplay influences the mind of the spectator. If we try to understand and to explain the means by which music exerts its powerful effects, we do not reach our goal by describing the structure of the piano and of the violin, or by explaining the physical laws of sound. We must proceed to the psychology and ask for the mental processes of the hearing of tones and of chords, of harmonies and disharmonies, of tone qualities and tone intensities, of rhythms and phrases, and must trace how these elements are combined in the melodies and compositions. In this way, we turn to the photoplay, at first with a purely psychological interest, and ask for the elementary excitements of the mind which enter into our experience of the moving pictures. We now disregard entirely the idea of the theater performance. We should block our way if we were to start from the theater and were to ask how much is left out in the mere photographic substitute. We approach the art of the film theater as if it stood entirely on its own ground, and extinguish all memory of the world of actors. We analyze the mental processes which this specific form of artistic endeavor produces in us.

To begin at the beginning, the photoplay consists of a series of flat pictures in contrast to the plastic objects of the real world which surrounds us. But we may stop at once: what does it mean to say that the surroundings appear to the mind plastic and the moving pictures flat? The psychology of this difference is easily misunderstood. Of course, when we are sitting in the picture palace, we know that we see a flat screen and that the object which we see has only two dimensions, right-left, and up-down, but not the third dimension of depth, of distance toward us or away from us. It is flat like a picture and never plastic like a work of sculpture or architecture or like a stage. Yet this is knowledge and not immediate impression. We have no right whatever to say that the scenes which we see on the screen appear to us as flat pictures.

We may become more strongly conscious of this difference between an object of our knowledge and an object of our impression, if we remember a well-known instrument, the stereoscope. The stereoscope, which was quite familiar to the parlor of a former generation, consists of two prisms through which the two eyes look toward two photographic views of a landscape. But the two photographic views are not identical. The landscape is taken from two different points of view, once from the right and once from the left. As soon as these two views are put into the stereoscope the right eye sees through the prism only the view from the right, the left eye only the view from the left. We know very well that only two flat pictures are before us; yet we cannot help seeing the landscape in strongly plastic forms. The two different views are combined in one presentation of the landscape in which the distant objects appear much further away from us than the foreground. We feel immediately the depth of things. It is as if we were looking at a small plastic model of the landscape and, in spite of our objective knowledge, cannot recognize the flat pictures in the solid forms which we perceive. It cannot be otherwise, because whenever in practical life we see an object, a vase on our table, as a solid body, we get the impression of its plastic character first of all by seeing it with our two eyes from two different points of view. The perspective in which our right eye sees the things on our table is different from the perspective for the left eye. Our plastic seeing therefore depends upon this combination of two different perspective views, and whenever we offer to the two eyes such one-sided views, they must be combined into the impression of the substantial thing. The stereoscope thus illustrates clearly that the knowledge of the flat character of pictures by no means excludes the actual perception of depth, and the question arises whether the moving pictures of the photoplay, in spite of our knowledge concerning the flatness of the screen, do not give us after all the impression of actual depth.

It may be said offhand that even the complete appearance of depth such as the stereoscope offers would be in no way contradictory to the idea of moving pictures. Then the photoplay would give the same plastic impression which the real stage offers. All that would be needed is this. When the actors play the scenes, not a single but a double camera would have to take the pictures. Such a double camera focuses the scene from two different points of view, corresponding to the position of the two eyes. Both films are then to be projected on the screen at the same time by a double projection apparatus which secures complete correspondence of the two pictures, so that in every instance the left and the right view are overlapping on the screen. This would give, of course, a chaotic, blurring image. But if the apparatus which projects the left side view has a green glass in front of the lens and the one which projects the right side view a red glass, and every person in the audience has a pair of spectacles with the left glass green and the right glass red—a cardboard lorgnette with red and green gelatine paper would do the same service and costs only a few cents—the left eye would see only the left view, the right eye only the right view. We could not see the red lines through the green glass nor the green lines through the red glass. In the moment the left eye gets the left side view only and the right eye the right side view, the whole chaos of lines on the screen is organized, and we see the pictured room on the screen with the same depth as if it were really a solid room set on the stage and as if the rear wall in the room were actually ten or twenty feet behind the furniture in the front. The effect is so striking that no one can overcome the feeling of depth under these conditions.

But while the regular motion pictures certainly do not offer us this complete plastic impression, it would simply be the usual confusion between knowledge about the picture and its real appearance if we were to deny that we get a certain impression of depth. If several persons move in a room, we gain distinctly the feeling that one moves behind another in the film picture. They move toward us and from us just as much as they move to the right and left. We actually perceive the chairs or the rear wall of the room as further away from us than the persons in the foreground. This is not surprising if we stop to think how we perceive the depth, for instance, of a real stage. Let us fancy that we sit in the orchestra of a real theater and see before us the stage set as a room with furniture and persons in it. We now see the different objects on the stage at different distances, some near, some far. One of the causes was just mentioned. We see everything with our right or our left eye from different points of view. But if now we close one eye and look at the stage with the right eye only, the plastic effect does not disappear. The psychological causes for this perception of depth with one eye are essentially the differences of apparent size, the perspective relations, the shadows, and the actions performed in the space. Now all these factors which help us to grasp the furniture on the stage as solid and substantial play their role no less in the room which is projected on the screen.

We are too readily inclined to imagine that our eye can directly grasp the different distances in our surroundings. Yet we need only imagine that a large glass plate is put in the place of the curtain covering the whole stage. Now we see the stage through the glass; and if we look at it with one eye only it is evident that every single spot on the stage must throw its light to our eye by light rays which cross the glass plate at a particular point. For our seeing it would make no difference whether the stage is actually behind that glass plate or whether all the light rays which pass through the plate come from the plate itself. If those rays with all their different shades of light and dark started from the surface of the glass plate, the effect on the one eye would necessarily be the same as if they originated at different distances behind the glass. This is exactly the case of the screen. If the pictures are well taken and the projection is sharp and we sit at the right distance from the picture, we must have the same impression as if we looked through a glass plate into a real space.

The photoplay is therefore poorly characterized if the flatness of the pictorial view is presented as an essential feature. That flatness is an objective part of the technical physical arrangements, but not a feature of that which we really see in the performance of the photoplay. We are there in the midst of a three-dimensional world, and the movements of the persons or of the animals or even of the lifeless things, like the streaming of the water in the brook or the movements of the leaves in the wind, strongly maintain our immediate impression of depth. Many secondary features characteristic of the motion picture may help. For instance, by a well-known optical illusion the feeling of depth is strengthened if the foreground is at rest and the background moving. Thus the ship passing in front of the motionless background of the harbor by no means suggests depth to the same degree as the picture taken on the gliding ship itself so that the ship appears to be at rest and the harbor itself passing by.

The depth effect is so undeniable that some minds are struck by it as the chief power in the impressions from the screen. Vachel Lindsay, the poet, feels the plastic character of the persons in the foreground so fully that he interprets those plays with much individual action as a kind of sculpture in motion. He says: "The little far off people on the old-fashioned speaking stage do not appeal to the plastic sense in this way. They are by comparison mere bits of pasteboard with sweet voices, while on the other hand the photoplay foreground is full of dumb giants. The bodies of these giants are in high sculptural relief." Others have emphasized that this strong feeling of depth touches them most when persons in the foreground stand with a far distant landscape as background—much more than when they are seen in a room. Psychologically, this is not surprising either. If the scene were a real room, every detail in it would appear differently to the two eyes. In the room on the screen, both eyes receive the same impression, and the result is that the consciousness of depth is inhibited. But when a far distant landscape is the only background, the impression from the picture and life is indeed the same. The trees or mountains which are several hundred feet distant from the eye give to both eyes exactly the same impression, inasmuch as the small difference of position between the two eyeballs has no influence compared with the distance of the objects from our face. We would see the mountains with both eyes alike in reality, and therefore we feel unhampered in our subjective interpretation of far distant vision when the screen offers exactly the same picture of the mountains to our two eyes. Hence in such cases we believe that we see the persons really in the foreground and the landscape far away.

Nevertheless we are never deceived; we are fully conscious of the depth, and yet we do not take it for real depth. Too much stands in the way. Some unfavorable conditions are still deficiencies of the technique; for instance, the camera picture in some respects exaggerates the distances. If we see through the open door of the rear wall into one or two other rooms, they appear like a distant corridor. Moreover, we have ideal conditions for vision in the right perspective only when we sit in front of the screen at a definite distance. We ought to sit where we see the objects in the picture at the same angle at which the camera photographed the originals. If we are too near or too far or too much to one side, we perceive the plastic scene from a viewpoint which would demand an entirely different perspective than that which the camera fixated. In motionless pictures this is less disturbing; in moving pictures every new movement to or from the background must remind us of the apparent distortion. Moreover, the size and the frame and the whole setting strongly remind us of the unreality of the perceived space. But the chief point remains that we see the whole picture with both eyes and not with only one, and that we are constantly reminded of the flatness of the picture because the two eyes receive identical impressions. And we may add an argument nearly related to it, namely, that the screen as such is an object of our perception and demands an adaptation of the eye and an independent localization. We are drawn into this conflict of perception even when we look into a mirror. If we stand three feet from a large mirror on the wall, we see our reflection three feet from our eyes in the plate glass, and we see it at the same time six feet from our eye behind the glass. Both localizations take hold of our mind and produce a peculiar interference. We all have learned to ignore it, but characteristic illusions remain which indicate the reality of this doubleness.

In the case of the picture on the screen this conflict is much stronger. *We certainly see the depth, and yet we cannot accept it.* There is too much which inhibits belief and interferes with the interpretation of the people and landscape before us as truly plastic. They are surely not simply pictures. The persons can move toward us and away from us, and the river flows into a distant valley. And yet the distance in which the people move is not the distance of our real space, such as the theater shows, and the persons themselves are not flesh and blood. It is a unique inner experience, which is characteristic of the perception of the photoplays. *We have reality with all its true dimensions; and yet it keeps the fleeting, passing surface suggestion without true depth and fullness, as different from a mere picture as from a mere stage performance.* It brings our mind into a peculiar complex state, and we shall see that this plays a not unimportant part in the mental make-up of the whole photoplay.

While the problem of depth in the film picture is easily ignored, the problem of movement forces itself on every spectator. It seems as if here the really essential trait of the film performance is to be found, and that the explanation of the motion in the pictures is the chief task which the psychologist must meet. We know that any single picture which the film of the photographer has fixed is immovable. We know, furthermore, that we do not see the passing by of the long strip of film. We know that it is rolled from one roll and rolled up on another, but that this movement from picture to picture is not visible. It goes on while the field is darkened. What objectively reaches our eye is one motionless picture after another, but the replacing of one by another through a forward movement of the film cannot reach our eye at all. Why do we, nevertheless, see a continuous movement? The problem did not arise with the kinetoscope only but had interested the preceding generations who amused themselves with the phenakistoscope and the stroboscopic disks or the magic cylinder of the zoötrope and bioscope. The child who made his zoötrope revolve and looked through the slits of the black cover in the drum saw through every slit the drawing of a dog in one particular position. Yet as the twenty-four slits passed the eye, the twenty-four different positions blended into one continuous jumping movement of the poodle.

But this so-called stroboscopic phenomenon, however interesting it was, seemed to offer hardly any difficulty. The friends of the zoötrope surely knew another little plaything, the thaumatrope. Dr. Paris had invented it in 1827. It shows two pictures, one on the front, one on the rear side of a card. As soon as the card is quickly revolved about a central axis, the two pictures fuse into one. If a horse is on one side and a rider on the other, if a cage is on one and a bird on the other, we see the rider on the horse and the bird in the cage. It cannot be otherwise. It is simply the result of the positive afterimages. If, at dark, we twirl a glowing joss stick in a circle, we do not see one point moving from place to place, but we see a continuous circular line. It is nowhere broken because, if the movement is quick, the positive after-image of the light in its first position is still effective in our eye when the glowing point has passed through the whole circle and has reached the first position again.

We speak of this effect as a positive afterimage, because it is a real continuation of the first impression and stands in contrast to the so-called negative afterimage in which the aftereffect is opposite to the original stimulus. In the case of a negative afterimage the light impression leaves a dark spot, the dark impression gives a light afterimage. Black becomes white and white becomes black; in the world of colors red leaves a green and green a red afterimage, yellow a blue and blue a yellow afterimage. If we look at the crimson sinking sun and then at a white wall, we do not see red light spots but green dark spots. Compared with these negative pictures, the positive afterimages are short and they last through any noticeable time only with rather intense illumination. Yet they are evidently sufficient to bridge the interval between the two slits in the stroboscopic disk or in the zoötrope, the interval in which the black paper passes the eye and in which accordingly no new stimulus reaches the nerves. The routine explanation of the appearance of movement was accordingly: that every picture of a particular position left in the eye an afterimage until the next picture with the slightly changed position of the jumping animal or of the marching men was in sight, and the afterimage of this again lasted until the third came. The afterimages were responsible for the fact that no interruptions were noticeable, while the movement itself resulted simply from the passing of one position into another. What else is the perception of movement but the seeing of a long series of different positions? If instead of looking through the zoötrope we watch a real

trotting horse on a real street, we see its whole body in ever new pro-
gressing positions and its legs in all phases of motion; and this continuous series is our perception of the movement itself.

This seems very simple. Yet it was slowly discovered that the explanation is far too simple and that it does not in the least do justice to the true experiences. With the advance of modern laboratory
psychology the experimental investigations frequently turned to the
analysis of our perception of movement. In the last thirty years many
researches, notably those of Stricker, Exner, Hull, James, Fischer,
Stern, Marbe, Lincke, Wertheimer, and Korte have thrown new light
on the problem by carefully devised experiments.[10] One result of them
came quickly into the foreground of the newer view: the perception
of movement is an independent experience which cannot be reduced
to a simple seeing of a series of different positions. A characteristic
content of consciousness must be added to such a series of visual
impressions. The mere idea of succeeding phases of movement is not
at all the original movement idea. This is suggested first by the various illusions of movement. We may believe that we perceive a movement where no actual changes of visual impressions occur. This, to be
sure, may result from a mere misinterpretation of the impression: for
instance when in the railway train at the station we look out of the
window and believe suddenly that our train is moving, while in reality
the train on the neighboring track has started. It is the same when we
see the moon floating quickly through the motionless clouds. We are
inclined to consider as being at rest that which we fixate and to interpret the relative changes in the field of vision as movements of those
parts which we do not fixate.

But it is different when we come, for instance, to those illusions in
which movement is forced on our perception by contrast and aftereffect. We look from a bridge into the flowing water and, if we turn
our eyes toward the land, the motionless shore seems to swim in the
opposite direction. It is not sufficient in such cases to refer to contrasting eye movements. It can easily be shown by experiments that
these movements and countermovements in the field of vision can

proceed in opposite directions at the same time, and no eye, of course, is able to move upward and downward, or right and left, in the same moment. A very characteristic experiment can be performed with a black spiral line on a white disk. If we revolve such a disk slowly around its center, the spiral line produces the impression of a continuous enlargement of concentric curves. The lines start at the center and expand until they disappear in the periphery. If we look for a minute or two into this play of the expanding curves and then turn our eyes to the face of a neighbor, we see at once how the features of the face begin to shrink. It looks as if the whole face were elastically drawn toward its center. If we revolve the disk in the opposite direction, the curves seem to move from the edge of the disk toward the center, becoming smaller and smaller, and if then we look toward a face, the person seems to swell up, and every point in the face seems to move from the nose toward the chin or forehead or ears. Our eye which watches such an aftereffect cannot really move at the same time from the center of the face toward both ears and the hair and the chin. The impression of movement must therefore have other conditions than the actual performance of the movements, and above all it is clear from such tests that the seeing of the movements is a unique experience which can be entirely independent from the actual seeing of successive positions. The eye itself gets the impression of a face at rest, and yet we see the face in the one case shrinking, in the other case swelling; in the one case every point apparently moving toward the center, in the other case apparently moving away from the center. The experience of movement is here evidently produced by the spectator's mind and not excited from without.

We may approach the same result also from experiments of a very different kind. If a flash of light at one point is followed by a flash at another point after a very short time, about a twentieth of a second, the two lights appear to us simultaneous. The first light is still fully visible when the second flashes, and it cannot be noticed that the second comes later than the first. If now, in the same short time interval, the first light moves toward the second point, we should expect that we would see the whole process as a lighted line at rest, inasmuch as the beginning and the end point appear simultaneous if the end is reached less than a twentieth of a second after the starting point. But the experiment shows the opposite result. Instead of the expected lighted line, we see in this case an actual movement from one point to the other. Again, we must conclude that the movement is more than the mere seeing of successive positions, as in this case we see the movement, while the isolated positions do not appear as successive but as simultaneous.

Another group of interesting phenomena of movement may be formed from those cases in which the moving object is more easily noticed than the impressions of the whole field through which the movement is carried out. We may overlook an area in our visual field, especially when it lies far to one side from our fixation point, but as soon as anything moves in that area our attention is drawn. We notice the movement more quickly than the whole background in which the movement is executed. The fluttering of kerchiefs at a far distance or the waving of flags for signaling is characteristic. All indicate that the movement is to us something different from merely seeing an object first at one and afterward at another place. We can easily find the analogy in other senses. If we touch our forehead or the back of our hand with two blunt compass points so that the two points are about a third of an inch distant from each other, we do not discriminate the two points as two, but we perceive the impression as that of one point. We cannot discriminate the one pressure point from the other. But if we move the point of a pencil to and fro from one point to the other we perceive distinctly the movement in spite of the fact that it is a movement between two end points which could not be discriminated. It is wholly characteristic that the experimenter in every field of sensations, visual or acoustical or tactual, often finds himself before the experience of having noticed a movement while he is unable to say in which direction the movement occurred.

We are familiar with the illusions in which we believe that we see something which only our imagination supplies. If an unfamiliar printed word is exposed to our eye for the twentieth part of a second, we readily substitute a familiar word with similar letters. Everybody knows how difficult it is to read proofs. We overlook the misprints, that is, we replace the wrong letters which are actually in our field of vision by imaginary right letters which correspond to our expectations. Are we not also familiar with the experience of supplying, by our fancy, the associative image of a movement when only the starting point and the end point are given if a skillful suggestion influences our mind? The prestidigitator stands on one side of the stage when he apparently throws the costly watch against the mirror on the other side of the stage; the audience sees his suggestive hand movement and the disappearance of the watch and sees twenty feet away the shattering of the mirror. The suggestible spectator cannot help seeing the flight of the watch across the stage.

The recent experiments by Wertheimer and Korte have gone into still subtler details. Both experimenters worked with a delicate instrument in which two light lines on a dark ground could be exposed in very quick succession and in which it was possible to vary the position of the lines, the distance of the lines, the intensity of their light, the time exposure of each, and the time between the appearance of the first and of the second. They studied all these factors, and moreover the influence of differently directed attention and suggestive attitude. If a vertical line is immediately followed by a horizontal, the two together may give the impression of one right angle. If the time between the vertical and the horizontal line is long, first one and then the other is seen. But at a certain length of the time interval, a new effect is reached. We see the vertical line falling over and lying flat like the horizontal line. If the eyes are fixed on the point in the midst of the angle, we might expect that this movement phenomenon would stop, but the opposite is the case. The apparent movement from the vertical to the horizontal has to pass our fixation point, and it seems that we ought now to recognize clearly that there is nothing between those two positions, that the intermediate phases of the movement are lacking; and yet the experiment shows that, under these circumstances, we frequently get the strongest impression of motion. If we use two horizontal lines, the one above the other, we see, if the right time interval is chosen, that the upper one moves downward toward the lower. But we can introduce there a very interesting variation. If we make the lower line, which appears objectively after the upper one, more intense, the total impression is one which begins with the lower. We see first the lower line moving toward the upper one which also approaches the lower; and then follows the second phase in which both appear to fall down to the position of the lower one. It is not necessary to go further into details in order to demonstrate that the apparent movement is in no way the mere result of an afterimage and that the impression of motion is surely more than the mere perception of successive phases of movement. The movement is, in these cases, not really seen from without, but is superadded, by the action of the mind, to motionless pictures.

The statement that our impression of movement does not result simply from the seeing of successive stages but includes a higher mental act into which the successive visual impressions enter merely as factors is in itself not really an explanation. We have not settled by it the nature of that higher central process. But it is enough for us to see that the impression of the continuity of the motion results from a complex mental process by which the various pictures are held together in the unity of a higher act. Nothing can characterize the situation more clearly than the fact which has been demonstrated by many experiments, namely, that this feeling of movement is in no way interfered with by the distinct consciousness that important phases of the movement are lacking. On the contrary, under certain circumstances, we become still more fully aware of this apparent motion created by our inner activity when we are conscious of the interruptions between the various phases of movement.

We come to the consequences. What is then the difference between seeing motion in the photoplay and seeing it on the real stage? There on the stage where the actors move the eye really receives a continuous series. Each position goes over into the next without any interruption. The spectator receives everything from without and the whole movement which he sees is actually going on in the world of space without and, accordingly, in his eye. But if he faces the film world, *the motion which he sees appears to be a true motion, and yet is created by his own mind.* The afterimages of the successive pictures are not sufficient to produce a substitute for the continuous outer stimulation; the essential condition is rather the inner mental activity which unites the separate phases in the idea of connected action. Thus, we have reached the exact counterpart of our results when we analyzed the perception of depth. We see actual depth in the pictures, and yet we are every instant aware that it is not real depth and that the persons are not really plastic. It is only a suggestion of depth, a depth created by our own activity, but not actually seen, because essential conditions for the true perception of depth are lacking. Now we find that the movement too is perceived but that the eye does not receive the impressions of true movement. It is only a suggestion of movement, and the idea of motion is to a high degree the product of our own reaction. *Depth and movement alike come to us in the moving picture world, not as hard facts but as a mixture of fact and symbol. They are present and yet they are not in the things. We invest the impressions with them.* The theater has both depth and motion, without any subjective help; the screen has them and yet lacks them. We see things distant and moving, but we furnish to them more than we receive; we create the depth and the continuity through our mental mechanism.

Chapter 4: **Attention**

The mere perception of the men and women and of the background, with all their depth and their motion, furnishes only the material. The scene which keeps our interest alive certainly involves much more than the simple impression of moving and distant objects. We must accompany those sights with a wealth of ideas. They must have a meaning for us, they must be enriched by our own imagination, they must awaken the remnants of earlier experiences, they must stir up our feelings and emotions, they must play on our suggestibility, they must start ideas and thoughts, they must be linked in our mind with the continuous chain of the play, and they must draw our attention constantly to the important and essential element of the action. An abundance of such inner processes must meet the world of impressions and the psychological analysis has only started when perception of depth and movement alone are considered. If we hear Chinese, we perceive the sounds, but there is no inner response to the words; they are meaningless and dead for us; we have no interest in them. If we hear the same thoughts expressed in our mother tongue, every syllable carries its meaning and message. Then we are readily inclined to fancy that this additional significance which belongs to the familiar language and which is absent from the foreign one is something which comes to us in the perception itself as if the meaning too were passing through the channels of our ears. But psychologically the meaning is ours. In learning the language, we have learned to add associations and reactions of our own to the sounds which we perceive. It is not different with the optical perceptions. The best does not come from without.

Of all internal functions that create the meaning of the world around us, the most central is the attention. The chaos of the surrounding impressions is organized into a real cosmos of experience by our selection of that which is significant and of consequence. This is true for life and stage alike. Our attention must be drawn now here, now there, if we want to bind together that which is scattered in the space before us. Everything must be shaded by attention and inattention. Whatever is focused by our attention wins emphasis and irradiates meaning over the course of events. In practical life, we discriminate between voluntary and involuntary attention. We call it voluntary if we approach the impressions with an idea in our mind as to what we want to focus our attention on. We carry our personal interest, our own idea into the observation of the objects. Our attention has chosen its aim beforehand, and we ignore all that does not fulfil this specific interest. All our working is controlled by such voluntary attention. We have the idea of the goal which we want to reach in our mind beforehand and subordinate all which we meet to this selective energy. Through our voluntary attention we seek something and accept the offering of the surroundings only in so far as it brings us what we are seeking.

It is quite different with the involuntary attention. The guiding influence here comes from without. The cue for the focusing of our attention lies in the events which we perceive. What is loud and shining and unusual attracts our involuntary attention. We must turn our mind to a place where an explosion occurs, we must read the glaring electric signs which flash up. To be sure, the perceptions which force themselves on our involuntary attention may get their motive power from our own reactions. Everything which appeals to our natural instincts, everything which stirs up hope or fear, enthusiasm or indignation, or any strong emotional excitement will get control of our attention. But in spite of this circuit through our emotional responses the starting point lies without, and our attention is accordingly of the involuntary type. In our daily activity, voluntary and involuntary attention are always intertwined. Our life is a great compromise between that which our voluntary attention aims at and that which the aims of the surrounding world force on our involuntary attention.

How does the theater performance differ in this respect from life? Might we not say that voluntary attention is eliminated from the sphere of art and that the audience is necessarily following the lead of an attention which receives all its cues from the work of art itself and which therefore acts involuntarily? To be sure, we may approach a theater performance with a voluntary purpose of our own. For instance, we may be interested in a particular actor and may watch him with our opera glass all the time whenever he is on the stage, even in scenes in which his role is insignificant and in which the artistic interest ought to belong to the other actors. But such voluntary selection has evidently nothing to do with the theater performance as such. By such behavior we break the spell in which the artistic drama ought to hold us. We disregard the real shadings of the play, and by mere personal side interests, put emphasis where it does not belong. If we really enter into the spirit of the play, our attention is constantly drawn in accordance with the intentions of the producers.

Surely, the theater has no lack of means to draw this involuntary attention to any important point. To begin with, the actor who speaks holds our attention more strongly than the actors who at that time are silent. Yet the contents of the words may direct our interest to anybody else on the stage. We watch him whom the words accuse, or betray, or delight. But the mere interest springing from words cannot in the least explain that constantly shifting action of our involuntary attention during a theater performance. The movements of the actors are essential. The pantomime without words can take the place of the drama and still appeal to us with overwhelming power. The actor who comes to the foreground of the stage is at once in the foreground of our consciousness. He who lifts his arm while the others stand quiet has gained our attention. Above all, every gesture, every play of the features, brings order and rhythm into the manifoldness of the impressions and organizes them for our mind. Again, the quick action, the unusual action, the repeated action, the unexpected action, the action with strong outer effect, will force itself on our mind and unbalance the mental equilibrium.

The question arises: how does the photoplay secure the needed shifting of attention? Here, too, involuntary attention alone can be expected. An attention which undertakes its explorations guided by preconceived ideas instead of yielding to the demands of the play would lack adjustment to its task. We might sit through the photoplay with the voluntary intention of watching the pictures with a scientific interest, in order to detect some mechanical traits of the camera, or with a practical interest, in order to look up some new fashions, or with a professional interest, in order to find out in what New England scenery these pictures of Palestine might have been photographed. But none of these aspects has anything to do with the photoplay. If we follow the play in a genuine attitude of theatrical interest, we must accept those cues for our attention which the playwright and the producers have prepared for us. But there is surely no lack of means by which our mind can be influenced and directed in the rapid play of the pictures.

Of course the spoken word is lacking. We know how often the words on the screen serve as substitutes for the speech of the actors. They appear sometimes as so-called "leaders" between the pictures, sometimes even thrown into the picture itself, sometimes as content of a written letter or of a telegram or of a newspaper clipping which is projected like a picture, strongly enlarged, on the screen. In all these cases, the words themselves prescribe the line in which the attention must move and force the interest of the spectator toward the new goal. But such help by the writing on the wall is, after all, extraneous to the original character of the photoplay. As long as we study the psychological effect of the moving pictures themselves, we must concentrate our inquiry on the moving pictures as such and not on that which the playwright does for the interpretation of the pictures. It may be granted that the letters and newspaper articles take a middle place. They are a part of the picture, but their influence on the spectator is, nevertheless, very similar to that of the leaders. We are here concerned only with what the pictorial offering contains. We must, therefore, also disregard the accompanying music or the imitative noises which belong to the technique of the full-fledged photoplay nowadays. They do not a little to push the attention hither and thither. Yet they are accessory, while the primary power must lie in the content of the pictures themselves.

But it is evident that with the exception of the words, no means for drawing attention which is effective on the theater stage is lost in the photoplay. All the directing influences which the movements of the actors exert can be felt no less when they are pictured in the films. More than that, the absence of the words brings the movements which we see to still greater prominence in our mind. Our whole attention can now be focused on the play of the face and of the hands. Every gesture and every mimic excitement stirs us now much more than if it were only the accompaniment of speech. Moreover, the technical conditions of the kinematograph show favor the importance of the movement. First the play on the screen is acted more rapidly than that on the stage. By the absence of speech, everything is condensed, the whole rhythm is quickened, a greater pressure of time is applied, and through that the accents become sharper and the emphasis more powerful for the attention. But secondly, the form of the stage intensifies the impression made by those who move toward the foreground. The theater stage is broadest near the footlights and becomes narrower toward the background; the moving picture stage is narrowest in front and becomes wider toward the background. This is necessary because its width is controlled by the angle at which the camera takes the picture. The camera is the apex of an angle which encloses a breadth of only a few feet in the nearest photographic distance, while it may include a width of miles in the far distant landscape. Whatever comes to the foreground therefore gains strongly in relative importance over its surroundings. Moving away from the camera means a reduction much greater than a mere stepping to the background on the theater stage. Furthermore lifeless things have much more chance for movements in the moving pictures than on the stage, and their motions, too, can contribute toward the right setting of the attention.

But we know from the theater that movement is not the only condition which makes us focus our interest on a particular element of the play. An unusual face, a queer dress, a gorgeous costume or a surprising lack of costume, a quaint piece of decoration, may attract our mind and even hold it spellbound for a while. Such means cannot only be used but can be carried to a much stronger climax of efficiency by the unlimited means of the moving pictures. This is still more true of the power of setting or background. The painted landscape of the stage can hardly compete with the wonders of nature and culture when the scene of the photoplay is laid in the supreme landscapes of the world. Wide vistas are opened, the woods and the streams, the mountain valleys and the ocean, are before us with the whole strength of reality; and yet in rapid change which does not allow the attention to become fatigued.

Finally the mere formal arrangement of the succeeding pictures may keep our attention in control, and here again are possibilities which are superior to those of the solid theater stage. At the theater, no effect of formal arrangement can give exactly the same impression to the spectators in every part of the house. The perspective of the wings and the other settings and their relation to the persons and to the background can never appear alike from the front and from the rear, from the left and from the right side, from the orchestra and from the balcony, while the picture which the camera has fixated is the same from every corner of the picture palace. The greatest skill and refinement can be applied to make the composition serviceable to the needs of attention. The spectator may not and ought not to be aware that the lines of the background, the hangings of the room, the curves of the furniture, the branches of the trees, the forms of the mountains, help to point toward the figure of the woman who is to hold his mind. The shading of the lights, the patches of dark shadows, the vagueness of some parts, the sharp outlines of others, the quietness of some parts of the picture as against the vehement movement of others all play on the keyboard of our mind and secure the desired effect on our involuntary attention.

But if all is admitted, we still have not touched on the most important and most characteristic relation of the photoplay pictures to the attention of the audience; and here we reach a sphere in which any comparison with the stage of the theater would be in vain. What is attention? What are the essential processes in the mind when we turn our attention to one face in the crowd, to one little flower in the wide landscape? It would be wrong to describe the process in the mind by reference to one change alone. If we have to give an account of the act of attention, as seen by the modern psychologist, we ought to point to several coordinated features. They are not independent of one another but are closely interrelated. We may say that whatever attracts our attention in the sphere of any sense, sight or sound, touch or smell, surely becomes more vivid and more clear in our consciousness. This does not at all mean that it becomes more intense. A faint light to which we turn our attention does not become the strong light of an incandescent lamp. No, it remains the faint, just perceptible streak of lightness, but it has grown more impressive, more distinct, more clear in its details, more vivid. It has taken a stronger hold of us or, as we may say by a metaphor, it has come into the center of our consciousness.

But this involves a second aspect which is surely no less important. While the attended impression becomes more vivid, all the other impressions become less vivid, less clear, less distinct, less detailed. They fade away. We no longer notice them. They have no hold on our mind, they disappear. If we are fully absorbed in our book, we do not hear at all what is said around us and we do not see the room; we forget everything. Our attention to the page of the book brings with it our lack of attention to everything else. We may add a third factor. We feel that our body adjusts itself to the perception. Our head enters into the movement of listening for the sound, our eyes are fixating the point in the outer world. We hold all our muscles in tension in order to receive the fullest possible impression with our sense organs. The lens in our eye is accommodated exactly to the correct distance. In short our bodily personality works toward the fullest possible impression. But this is supplemented by a fourth factor. Our ideas and feelings and impulses group themselves around the attended object. It becomes the starting point for our actions, while all the other objects in the sphere of our senses lose their grip on our ideas and feelings. These four factors are intimately related to one another. As we are passing along the street we see something in the shop window and as soon as it stirs up our interest, our body adjusts itself, we stop, we fixate it, we get more of the detail in it, the lines become sharper, and while it impresses us more vividly than before, the street around us has lost its vividness and clearness.

If on the stage the hand movements of the actor catch our interest, we no longer look at the whole large scene, we see only the fingers of the hero clutching the revolver with which he is to commit his crime. Our attention is entirely given up to the passionate play of his hand. It becomes the central point for all our emotional responses. We do not see the hands of any other actor in the scene. Everything else sinks into a general vague background, while that one hand shows more and more details. The more we fixate it, the more its clearness and distinctness increase. From this one point wells our emotion, and our emotion again concentrates our senses on this one point. It is as if this one hand were, during this pulse beat of events, the whole scene, and everything else had faded away. On the stage, this is impossible; there, nothing can really fade away. That dramatic hand must remain, after all, only the ten thousandth part of the space of the whole stage; it must remain a little detail. The whole body of the hero and the other men and the whole room and every indifferent chair and table in it must go on obtruding themselves on our senses. What we do not attend cannot be suddenly removed from the stage. Every change which is needed must be secured by our own mind. In our consciousness, the attended hand must grow and the surrounding room must blur. But the stage cannot help us. The art of the theater has there its limits.

Here begins the art of the photoplay. That one nervous hand which feverishly grasps the deadly weapon can suddenly for the space of a breath or two become enlarged and be alone visible on the screen, while everything else has really faded into darkness. The act of attention which goes on in our mind has remodeled the surrounding itself. The detail which is being watched has suddenly become the whole content of the performance, and everything which our mind wants to disregard has been suddenly banished from our sight and has disappeared. The events without have become obedient to the demands of our consciousness. In the language of the photoplay producers it is a "close-up." *The close-up has objectified in our world of perception our mental act of attention and by it has furnished art with a means which far transcends the power of any theater stage.*

The scheme of the close-up was introduced into the technique of the film play rather late, but it has quickly gained a secure position. The more elaborate the production, the more frequent and the more skillful the use of this new and artistic means. The melodrama can hardly be played without it, unless a most inartistic use of printed words is made. The close-up has to furnish the explanations. If a little locket is hung on the neck of the stolen or exchanged infant, it is not necessary to tell us in words that everything will hinge on this locket twenty years later when the girl is grown up. If the ornament at the child's throat is at once shown in a close-up where everything has disappeared and only its quaint form appears much enlarged on the screen, we fix it in our imagination and know that we must give our fullest attention to it, as it will play a decisive part in the next reel. The gentleman criminal who draws his handkerchief from his pocket and with it a little bit of paper which falls down on the rug unnoticed by him has no power to draw our attention to that incriminating scrap. The device hardly belongs in the theater because the audience would not notice it any more than would the scoundrel himself. It would not be able to draw the attention. But in the film it is a favorite trick. At the moment the bit of paper falls, we see it greatly enlarged on the rug, while everything else has faded away, and we read on it that it is a ticket from the railway station at which the great crime was committed. Our attention is focused on it, and we know that it will be decisive for the development of the action.

A clerk buys a newspaper on the street, glances at it and is shocked. Suddenly we see that piece of news with our own eyes. The close-up magnifies the headlines of the paper so that they fill the whole screen. But it is not necessary that this focusing of the attention should refer to levers in the plot. Any subtle detail, any significant gesture which heightens the meaning of the action may enter into the center of our consciousness by monopolizing the stage for a few seconds. There is love in her smiling face, and yet we overlook it as they stand in a crowded room. But suddenly, only for three seconds, all the others in the room have disappeared, the bodies of the lovers themselves have faded away, and only his look of longing and her smile of yielding reach out to us. The close-up has done what no theater could have offered by its own means, though we might have approached the effect in the theater performance if we had taken our opera glass and had directed it only to those two heads. But by doing so we should have emancipated ourselves from the offering of the stage picture, that is, the concentration and focusing were secured by us and not by the performance. In the photoplay, it is the opposite. Have we not reached by this analysis of the close-up a point very near to that to which the study of depth perception and movement perception was leading? We saw that the moving pictures give us the plastic world and the moving world, and that nevertheless the depth and the motion in it are not real, unlike the depth and motion of the stage. We find now that the reality of the action in the photoplay in still another respect lacks objective independence, because it yields to our subjective play of attention. Wherever our attention becomes focused on a special feature, the surrounding adjusts itself, eliminates everything in which we are not interested, and by the close-up heightens the vividness of that on which our mind is concentrated. It is as if that outer world were woven into our mind and were shaped not through its own laws but by the acts of our attention.

Chapter 5: **Memory and Imagination**

When we sit in a real theater and see the stage with its depth and watch the actors moving and turn our attention hither and thither, we feel that those impressions from behind the footlights have objective character, while the action of our attention is subjective. Those men and things come from without but the play of the attention starts from within. Yet our attention, as we have seen, does not really add anything to the impressions of the stage. It makes some more vivid and clear while others become vague or fade away, but through the attention alone no content enters our consciousness. Wherever our attention may wander on the stage, whatever we experience comes to us through the channels of our senses. The spectator in the audience, however, does experience more than merely the light and sound sensations which fall on the eye and ear at that moment. He may be entirely fascinated by the actions on the stage and yet his mind may be overflooded with other ideas. Only one of their sources, but not the least important one, is the memory.

Indeed the action of the memory brings to the mind of the audience ever so much which gives fuller meaning and ampler setting to every scene—yes, to every word and movement on the stage. To think of the most trivial case, at every point of the drama we must remember what happened in the previous scenes. The first act is no longer on the stage when we see the second. The second alone is now our sense impression. Yet this second act is in itself meaningless if it is not supported by the first. Hence the first must somehow be in our consciousness. At least in every important scene we must remember those situations of the preceding act which can throw light on the new developments. We see the young missionary in his adventures on his perilous journey, and we remember how in the preceding act we saw him in his peaceful cottage surrounded by the love of his parents and sisters and how they mourned when he left them behind. The more exciting the dangers he passes through in the far distant land, the more strongly does our memory carry us back to the home scenes which we witnessed before. The theater cannot do more than suggest to our memory this looking backward. The young hero may call this reminiscence back to our consciousness by his speech and his prayer, and when he fights his way through the jungles of Africa and the savages attack him, the melodrama may put words into his mouth which force us to think fervently of those whom he has left behind. But, after all, it is our own material of memory ideas which supplies the picture. The theater cannot go further. The photoplay can. We see the jungle, we see the hero at the height of his danger; and suddenly there flashes upon the screen a picture of the past. For not more than two seconds does the idyllic New England scene slip into the exciting African events. When one deep breath is over we are stirred again by the event of the present. That home scene of the past flitted by just as a hasty thought of bygone days darts through the mind.

The modern photoartist makes use of this technical device in an abundance of forms. In his slang any going back to an earlier scene is called a "cut-back." The cut-back may have many variations and serve many purposes. But the one which we face here is psychologically the most interesting. We have really an objectivation of our memory function. The case of the cut-back is there quite parallel to that of the close-up. In the one, we recognize the mental act of attending, in the other we must recognize the mental act of remembering. *In both cases, the act which in the ordinary theater would go on in our mind alone is here in the photography projected into the pictures themselves. It is as if reality has lost its own continuous connection and become shaped by the demands of our soul.* It is as if the outer world itself became molded in accordance with our fleeting turns of attention or with our passing memory ideas.

It is only another version of the same principle when the course of events is interrupted by forward glances. The mental function involved is that of expectation or, when the expectation is controlled by our feelings, we may class it under the mental function of imagination. The melodrama shows us how the young millionaire wastes his nights in a dissipated life, and when he drinks his blasphemous toast at a champagne feast with shameless women, we suddenly see on the screen the vision of twenty years later when the bartender of a most miserable saloon pushes the penniless tramp out into the gutter. The last act in the theater may bring us to such an ending, but there it can come only in the regular succession of events. That pitiful ending cannot be shown to us when life is still blooming and when a twenty years' downward course is still to be interpreted. There, only our own imagination can anticipate how the mill of life may grind. In the photoplay, our imagination is projected on the screen. With an uncanny contrast that ultimate picture of defeat breaks in where victory seems most glorious, and five seconds later the story of youth and rapture streams on. Again, we see the course of the natural events remolded by the power of the mind. The theater can picture only how the real occurrences might follow one another; the photoplay can overcome the interval of the future as well as the interval of the past and slip the day twenty years hence between this minute and the next. In short, it can act as our imagination acts. It has the mobility of our ideas which are not controlled by the physical necessity of outer events but by the psychological laws for the association of ideas. In our mind past and future become intertwined with the present. The photoplay obeys the laws of the mind rather than those of the outer world.

But the play of memory and imagination can have a still richer significance in the art of the film. The screen may produce not only what we remember or imagine but what the persons in the play see in their own minds. The technique of the camera stage has successfully introduced a distinct form for this kind of picturing. If a person in the scene remembers the past, a past which may be entirely unknown to the spectator but which is living in the memory of the hero or heroine, then the former events are not thrown on the screen as an entirely new set of pictures, but they are connected with the present scene by a slow transition. He sits at the fireplace in his study and receives the letter with the news of her wedding. The close-up picture which shows us the enlargement of the engraved wedding announcement appears as an entirely new picture. The room suddenly disappears and the hand which holds the card flashes up. Again, when we have read the card, it suddenly disappears, and we are in the room again. But when he has dreamily stirred the fire and sits down and gazes into the flames, then the room seems to dissolve, the lines blur, the details fade away, and while the walls and the whole room slowly melt, with the same slow transition the flower garden blossoms out, the flower garden where he and she sat together under the lilac bush and he confessed to her his boyish love. And then the garden slowly vanishes, and through the flowers we see once more the dim outlines of the room, and they become sharper and sharper until we are in the midst of the study again, and nothing is left of the vision of the past.

The technique of manufacturing such gradual transitions from one picture into another and back again demands much patience and is more difficult than the sudden change, as two exactly corresponding sets of views have to be produced and finally combined. But this cumbersome method has been fully accepted in moving picture making and the effect indeed somewhat symbolizes the appearance and disappearance of a reminiscence.

This scheme naturally opens wide perspectives. The skillful photoplaywright can communicate to us long scenes and complicated developments of the past in the form of such retrospective pictures. The man who shot his best friend has not offered an explanation in the court trial which we witness. It remains a perfect secret to the town and a mystery to the spectator, and now as the jail door closes behind him, the walls of the prison fuse and melt away, and we witness the scene in the little cottage where his friend secretly met his wife, and how he broke in, and how it all came about, and how he rejected every excuse which would dishonor his home. The whole murder story becomes embedded in the reappearance of his memory ideas. The effect is much less artistic when the photoplay, as not seldom happens, uses this pattern as a mere substitute for words. In the picturization of a Gaboriau story, the woman declines to tell before the court her life story which ended in a crime. She finally yields; she begins under oath to describe her whole past, and at the moment when she opens her mouth, the courtroom disappears and fades into the scene in which the love adventure began. Then we pass through a long set of scenes which lead to the critical point, and at that moment, we slide back into the courtroom and the woman finishes her confession. That is an external substitution of the pictures for the words, aesthetically on a much lower level than the other case, where the past was living only in the memory of the witness. Yet it is again an embodiment of past events which the genuine theater could offer to the ear but never to the eye.

Just as we can follow the reminiscences of the hero, we may share the fancies of his imagination. Once more the case is distinctly different from the one in which we, the spectators, had our imaginative ideas realized on the screen. Here we are passive witnesses to the wonders which are unveiled through the imagination of the persons in the play. We see the boy who is to enter the navy and who sleeps on shipboard the first night; the walls disappear and his imagination flutters from port to port. All he has seen in the pictures of foreign lands and has heard from his comrades becomes the background of his jubilant adventures. Now he stands in the rigging while the proud vessel sails into the harbor of Rio de Janeiro, and now into Manila Bay; now he enjoys himself in Japanese ports, and now by the shores of India; now he glides through the Suez Canal, and now he returns to the skyscrapers of New York. Not more than one minute was needed for his world travel in beautiful fantastic pictures, and yet we lived through all the boy's hopes and ecstasies with him. If we had seen the young sailor in his hammock on the theater stage, he might have hinted to us whatever passed through his mind by a kind of monologue or by some enthusiastic speech to a friend. But then we should have seen before our inner eye only that which the names of foreign places awake in ourselves. We should not really have seen the wonders of the world through the eyes of his soul and with the glow of his hope.

The drama would have given dead names to our ear; the photoplay gives ravishing scenery to our eye and shows the fancy of the young fellow in the scene really living.

From here we see the perspective to the fantastic dreams which the camera can fixate. Whenever the theater introduces an imagined setting and the stage clouds sink over the sleeper and the angels fill the stage, the beauty of the verses must excuse the shortcomings of the visual appeal. The photoplay artist can gain his triumphs here. Even the vulgar effects become softened by this setting. The ragged tramp who climbs a tree and falls asleep in the shady branches and then lives through a reversed world in which he and his kind feast and glory and live in palaces and sail in yachts, and, when the boiler of the yacht explodes, falls from the tree to the ground, becomes a tolerable spectacle because all is merged in the unreal pictures. Or, to think of the other extreme, gigantic visions of mankind crushed by the juggernaut of war and then blessed by the angel of peace may arise before our eyes with all their spiritual meaning.

Even the whole play may find its frame in a setting which offers a five-reel performance as one great imaginative dream. In the pretty play, *When Broadway Was a Trail*, the hero and heroine stand on the Metropolitan Tower and bend over its railing. They see the turmoil of New York of the present day and ships passing the Statue of Liberty. He begins to tell her of the past when, in the seventeenth century, Broadway was a trail, and suddenly the time which his imagination awakens is with us. Through two hours we follow the happenings of three hundred years ago. From New Amsterdam, it leads to the New England shores, all the early colonial life shows us its intimate charm, and when the hero has found his way back over the Broadway trail, we awake and see the last gestures with which the young narrator shows to the girl Broadway buildings of today.

Memory looks toward the past, expectation and imagination toward the future. But in the midst of the perception of our surroundings our mind turns not only to that which has happened before and which may happen later; it is interested in happenings at the same time in other places. The theater can show us only the events at one spot. Our mind craves more. Life does not move forward on one single pathway. The whole manifoldness of parallel currents with their endless interconnections is the true substance of our understanding. It may be the task of a particular art to force all into one steady development between the walls of one room, but every letter and every telephone call to the room remind us, even then, that other developments with other settings are proceeding in the same instant. The soul longs for this whole interplay, and the richer it is in contrasts, the more satisfaction may be drawn from our simultaneous presence in many quarters. The photoplay alone gives us our chance for such omnipresence. We see the banker, who had told his young wife that he has a directors' meeting, at a late hour in a cabaret feasting with a stenographer from his office. She had promised her poor old parents to be home early. We see the gorgeous roof garden and the tango dances, but our dramatic interest is divided among the frivolous pair, the jealous young woman in the suburban cottage, and the anxious old people in the attic. Our mind wavers among the three scenes. The photoplay shows one after another. Yet it can hardly be said that we think of them as successive. It is as if we were really at all three places at once. We see the joyous dance which is of central dramatic interest for twenty seconds, then for three seconds the wife in her luxurious boudoir looking at the dial of the clock, for three seconds again the grieved parents eagerly listening for any sound on the stairs, and anew for twenty seconds the turbulent festival. The frenzy reaches a climax, and in that moment we are suddenly again with his unhappy wife; it is only a flash, and the next instant we see the tears of the girl's poor mother. The three scenes proceed almost as if no one were interrupted at all. It is as if we saw one through another, as if three tones blended into one chord.

There is no limit to the number of threads which may be interwoven. A complex intrigue may demand cooperation at half a dozen spots, and we look now into one, now into another, and never have the impression that they come one after another. The temporal element has disappeared; the one action irradiates in all directions. Of course, this can easily be exaggerated, and the result must be a certain restlessness. If the scene changes too often and no movement is carried on without a break, the play may irritate us by its nervous jerking from place to place. Near the end of the Theda Bara edition of *Carmen* the scene changes one hundred and seventy times in ten minutes, an average of a little more than three seconds for each scene. We follow Don Jose and Carmen and the toreador in ever new phases of the dramatic action and are constantly carried back to Don Jose's home village where his mother waits for him. There, indeed, the dramatic tension has an element of nervousness, in contrast to the Geraldine Farrar version of *Carmen* which allows a more unbroken development of the single action.

But whether it is used with artistic reserve or with a certain dangerous exaggeration, in any case its psychological meaning is obvious. It demonstrates to us, in a new form, the same principle which the perception of depth and of movement, the acts of attention and of memory and of imagination have shown. *The objective world is molded by the interests of the mind. Events which are far distant from one another so that we could not be physically present at all of them at the same time are fusing in our field of vision, just as they are brought together in our own consciousness.* Psychologists are still debating whether the mind can ever devote itself to several groups of ideas at the same time. Some claim that any so-called division of attention is really a rapid alteration. Yet, in any case, subjectively we experience it as an actual division. Our mind is split and can be here and there apparently in one mental act. This inner division, this awareness of contrasting situations, this interchange of diverging experiences in the soul, can never be embodied except in the photoplay.

An interesting side light falls on this relation between the mind and the pictured scenes if we turn to a mental process which is quite nearly related to those which we have considered, namely, suggestion. It is similar in that a suggested idea which awakes in our consciousness is built up from the same material as the memory ideas or the imaginative ideas. The play of associations controls the suggestions, as it does the reminiscences and fancies. Yet, in an essential point, it is quite different. All the other associative ideas find merely their starting point in those outer impressions. We see a landscape on the stage or on the screen or in life and this visual perception is the cue which stirs up in our memory or imagination any fitting ideas. The choice of them, however, is completely controlled by our own interest and attitude and by our previous experiences. Those memories and fancies are, therefore, felt as our subjective supplements. We do not believe in their objective reality. A suggestion, on the other hand, is forced on us. The outer perception is not only a starting point but a controlling influence. The associated idea is not felt as our creation but as something to which we have to submit. The extreme case is, of course, that of the hypnotizer whose word awakens in the mind of the hypnotized person ideas which he cannot resist. He must accept them as real, he must believe that the dreary room is a beautiful garden in which he picks flowers.

The spellbound audience in a theater or in a picture house is certainly in a state of heightened suggestibility and is ready to receive suggestions. One great and fundamental suggestion is working in both cases, inasmuch as the drama, as well as the photoplay, suggests to the mind of the spectator that this is more than mere play, that it is life which we witness. But if we go further and ask for the application of suggestions in the detailed action, we cannot overlook the fact that the theater is extremely limited in its means. A series of events on the stage may strongly force on the mind the prediction of something which must follow, but inasmuch as the stage has to do with real physical beings who must behave according to the laws of nature, it cannot avoid offering us the actual events for which we were waiting. To be sure, even on the stage the hero may talk, the revolver in his hand, until it is fully suggested to us that the suicidal shot will end his life in the next instant, and yet just then the curtain may fall, and only the suggestion of his death may work in our mind. But this is evidently a very exceptional case as a fall of the curtain means the ending of the scene. In the act itself every series of events must come to its natural ending. If two men begin to fight on the stage, nothing remains to be suggested; we must simply witness the fight. And if two lovers embrace each other, we have to see their caresses.

The photoplay can not only "cut back" in the service of memories, but it can cut off in the service of suggestion. Even if the police did not demand that actual crimes and suicides should never be shown on the screen, for mere artistic reasons, it would be wiser to leave the climax to the suggestion to which the whole scene has led. There is no need of bringing the series of pictures to its logical end, because they are pictures only and not the real objects. At any instant, the man may disappear from the scene, and no automobile can race over the ground so rapidly that it cannot be stopped just as it is to crash into the rushing express train. The horseback rider jumps into the abyss; we see him fall, and yet, at the moment when he crashes to the ground, we are already in the midst of a far distant scene. Again and again, with doubtful taste, the sensuality of the nickel audiences has been stirred up by suggestive pictures of a girl undressing, and when in the intimate chamber the last garment was touched, the spectators were suddenly in the marketplace among crowds of people or in a sailing vessel on the river. The whole technique of the rapid changes of scenes, which we have recognized as so characteristic of photoplay, involves at every end point elements of suggestion which, to a certain degree, link the separate scenes as the afterimages link the separate pictures.

Chapter 6: **Emotions**

To picture emotions must be the central aim of the photoplay. In the drama, words of wisdom may be spoken, and we may listen to the conversations with interest even if they have only intellectual and not emotional character. But the actor whom we see on the screen can hold our attention only by what he is doing, and his actions gain meaning and unity for us through the feelings and emotions which control them. More than in the drama, the persons in the photoplay are to us, first of all, subjects of emotional experiences. Their joy and pain, their hope and fear, their love and hate, their gratitude and envy, their sympathy and malice, give meaning and value to the play. What are the chances of the photoartist to bring these feelings to a convincing expression?

No doubt, an emotion which is deprived of its discharge by words has lost a strong element, and yet gestures, actions, and facial play are so interwoven with the psychical process of an intense emotion that every shade can find its characteristic delivery. The face alone, with its tensions around the mouth, with its play of the eye, with its cast of the forehead, and even with the motions of the nostrils and the setting of the jaw, may bring numberless shades into the feeling tone. Here again the close-up can strongly heighten the impression. It is at the climax of emotion on the stage that the theatergoer likes to use his opera glass in order not to overlook the subtle excitement of the lips and the passion of the eyeballs and the ghastly pupil and the quivering cheeks. The enlargement by the close-up on the screen brings this emotional action of the face to sharpest relief. Or it may show us, enlarged, a play of the hands in which anger and rage or tender love or jealousy speak in unmistakable language. In humorous scenes, even the flirting of amorous feet may in the close-up tell the story of their possessors' hearts. Nevertheless there are narrow limits. Many emotional symptoms like blushing or growing pale would be lost in the mere photographic rendering, and, above all, these and many other signs of feeling are not under voluntary control. The photoactors may carefully go through the movements and imitate the contractions and relaxations of the muscles, and yet may be unable to produce those processes which are most essential for the true life emotion, namely those in the glands, blood vessels, and involuntary muscles.

Certainly the going through the motions will shade consciousness sufficiently so that some of these involuntary and instinctive responses may set in. The actor really experiences something of the inner excitement which he imitates, and with the excitement the automatic reactions appear. Yet only a few can actually shed tears, however much they move the muscles of the face into the semblance of crying. The pupil of the eye is somewhat more obedient, as the involuntary muscles of the iris respond to the cue which a strong imagination can give, and the mimic presentation of terror or astonishment or hatred may actually lead to the enlargement or contraction of the pupil, which the close-up may show. Yet there remains too much which mere art cannot render and which life alone produces, because the consciousness of the unreality of the situation works as a psychological inhibition on the automatic instinctive responses. The actor may artificially tremble, or breathe heavily, but the strong pulsation of the carotid artery or the moistness of the skin from perspiration will not come with an imitated emotion. Of course, that is true of the actor on the stage, too. But the content of the words and the modulation of the voice can help so much that the shortcomings of the visual impression are forgotten.

To the actor of the moving pictures, on the other hand, the temptation offers itself to overcome the deficiency by a heightening of the gestures and of the facial play, with the result that the emotional expression becomes exaggerated. No friend of the photoplay can deny that much of the photoart suffers from this almost unavoidable tendency. The quick marchlike rhythm of the drama of the reel favors this artificial overdoing, too. The rapid alternation of the scenes often seems to demand a jumping from one emotional climax to another, or rather the appearance of such extreme expressions where the content of the play hardly suggests such heights and depths of emotion. The soft lights are lost and the mental eye becomes adjusted to glaring flashes. This undeniable defect is felt with the American actors still more than with the European, especially with the French and Italian ones with whom excited gestures and highly accentuated expressions of the face are natural. A New England temperament forced into Neapolitan expressions of hatred or jealousy or adoration too easily appears a caricature. It is not by chance that so many strong actors of the stage are such more or less decided failures on the screen. They have been dragged into an art which is foreign to them, and their achievement has not seldom remained far below that of the specializing photoactor. The habitual reliance on the magic of the voice deprives them of the natural means of expression when they are to render emotions without words. They give too little or too much; they are not expressive, or they become grotesque.

Of course, the photoartist profits from one advantage. He is not obliged to find the most expressive gesture in one decisive moment of the stage performance. He can not only rehearse, but he can repeat the scene before the camera until exactly the right inspiration comes, and the manager who takes the close-up visage may discard many a poor pose before he strikes that one expression in which the whole content of the feeling of the scene is concentrated. In one other respect the producer of the photoplay has a technical advantage. More easily than the stage manager of the real theater, he can choose actors whose natural build and physiognomy fit the role and predispose them for the desired expression. The drama depends upon professional actors; the photoplay can pick players among any group of people for specific roles. They need no art of speaking and no training in delivery. The artificial make-up of the stage actors in order to give them special character is therefore less needed for the screen. The expression of the faces and the gestures must gain through such natural fitness of the man for the particular role. If the photoplay needs a brutal boxer in a mining camp, the producer will not, like the stage manager, try to transform a clean, neat, professional actor into a vulgar brute, but he will sift the Bowery until he has found some creature who looks as if he came from that mining camp and who has at least the prizefighter's cauliflower ear which results from the smashing of the ear cartilage. If he needs the fat bartender with his smug smile, or the humble Jewish peddler, or the Italian organ grinder, he does not rely on wigs and paint; he finds them all ready-made on the East Side. With the right body and countenance, the emotion is distinctly more credible. The emotional expression in the photoplays is therefore often more natural in the small roles which the outsiders play than in the chief parts of the professionals, who feel that they must outdo nature.

But our whole consideration so far has been one-sided and narrow. We have asked only about the means by which the photoactor expresses his emotion, and we were naturally confined to the analysis of his bodily reactions. But while the human individual in our surroundings has hardly any other means than the bodily expressions to show his emotions and moods, the photoplaywright is certainly not bound by these limits. Yet, even in life, the emotional tone may radiate beyond the body. A person expresses his mourning by his black clothes and his joy by gay attire, or he may make the piano or violin ring forth in happiness or moan in sadness. Even his whole room or house may be penetrated by his spirit of welcoming cordiality or his emotional setting of forbidding harshness. The feeling of the soul emanates into the surroundings, and the impressions which we get of our neighbor's emotional attitude may be derived from this external frame of the personality as much as from the gestures and the face.

This effect of the surrounding surely can and must be much heightened in the artistic theater play. All the stage settings of the scene ought to be in harmony with the fundamental emotions of the play, and many an act owes its success to the unity of emotional impression which results from the perfect painting of the background; it reverberates to the passions of the mind. From the highest artistic color and form effects of the stage in the Reinhardt style down to the cheapest melodrama with soft blue lights and tender music for the closing scene, the stage arrangements tell the story of the intimate emotion. But just this additional expression of the feeling through the medium of the surrounding scene, through background and setting, through lines and forms and movements, is very much more at the disposal of the photoartist. He alone can change the background and all the surroundings of the acting person from instant to instant. He is not bound to one setting, he has no technical difficulty in altering the whole scene with every smile and every frown. To be sure, the theater can give us changing sunshine and thunderclouds too. But it must go on at the slow pace and with the clumsiness with which the events in nature pass. The photoplay can flit from one to the other. Not more than one sixteenth of a second is needed to carry us from one corner of the globe to the other, from a jubilant setting to a mourning scene. The whole keyboard of the imagination may be used to serve this emotionalizing of nature.

There is a girl in her little room, and she opens a letter and reads it. There is no need of showing us in a close-up the letter page with the male handwriting and the words of love and the request for her hand. We see it in her radiant visage, we read it from her fascinated arms and hands; and yet how much more can the photoartist tell us about the storm of emotions in her soul. The walls of her little room fade away. Beautiful hedges of hawthorn blossom around her, rose bushes in wonderful glory arise, and the whole ground is alive with exotic flowers. Or the young artist sits in his attic playing his violin; we see the bow moving over the strings but the dreamy face of the player does not change with his music. Under the spell of his tones, his features are immovable as if they were staring at a vision. They do not speak of the changing emotions which his melodies awake. We cannot hear those tones. And yet we do hear them: a lovely spring landscape widens behind his head, we see the valleys of May and the bubbling brooks and the young wild beeches. And slowly it changes into the sadness of the autumn, the sere leaves are falling around the player, heavy clouds hang low over his head. Suddenly at a sharp accent of his bow the storm breaks, we are carried to the wildness of rugged rocks or to the raging sea; and again comes tranquillity over the world, the little country village of his youth fills the background, the harvest is brought from the fields, the sun sets upon a scene of happiness, and while the bow slowly sinks, the walls and ceiling of his attic close in again. No shade, no tint, no hue of his emotions has escaped us; we followed them as if we had heard the rejoicing and the sadness, the storm and the peace of his melodious tones. Such imaginative settings can be only the extreme; they would not be fit for the routine play. But, however much weaker and fainter the echo of the surroundings may be in the realistic pictures of the standard photoplay, the chances are abundant everywhere, and no skillful playwright will ever disregard them entirely. Not the portrait of the man but the picture as a whole has to be filled with emotional exuberance.

Everything so far has referred to the emotions of the persons in the play, but this cannot be sufficient. When we were interested in attention and memory, we did not ask about the act of attention and memory in the persons of the play, but in the spectator, and we recognized that these mental activities and excitements in the audience were projected into the moving pictures. Just here was the center of our interest, because it showed that uniqueness of the means with which the photoplaywright can work. If we want to shape the question now in the same way, we ought to ask how it is with the emotions of the spectator. But then, two different groups of cases must be distinguished. On the one side, we have those emotions in which the feelings of the persons in the play are transmitted to our own soul. On the other side, we find those feelings with which we respond to the scenes in the play, feelings which may be entirely different, perhaps exactly opposite to those which the figures in the play express.

The first group is by far the larger one. Our imitation of the emotions which we see expressed brings vividness and affective tone into our grasping of the play's action. We sympathize with the sufferer and that means that the pain which he expresses becomes our own pain. We share the joy of the happy lover and the grief of the despondent mourner, we feel the indignation of the betrayed wife and the fear of the man in danger. The visual perception of the various forms of expression of these emotions fuses in our mind with the conscious awareness of the emotion expressed; we feel as if we were directly seeing and observing the emotion itself. Moreover, the idea awakens in us the appropriate reactions. The horror which we see makes us really shrink, the happiness which we witness makes us relax, the pain which we observe brings contractions in our muscles; and all the resulting sensations from muscles, joints, tendons, from skin and viscera, from blood circulation and breathing, give the color of living experience to the emotional reflection in our mind. It is obvious that for this leading group of emotions the relation of the pictures to the feelings of the persons in the play and to the feelings of the spectator is exactly the same. If we start from the emotions of the audience, we can say that the pain and the joy which the spectator feels are really projected to the screen, projected both into the portraits of the persons and into the pictures of the scenery and background into which the personal emotions radiate. The fundamental principle which we recognized for all the other mental states is, accordingly, no less efficient in the case of the spectator's emotions.

The analysis of the mind of the audience must lead, however, to that second group of emotions, those in which the spectator responds to the scenes on the film from the standpoint of his independent affective life. We see an overbearing pompous person who is filled with the emotion of solemnity, and yet he awakens in us the emotion of humor. We answer by our ridicule. We see the scoundrel who in the melodramatic photoplay is filled with fiendish malice, and yet, we do not respond by imitating his emotion; we feel moral indignation toward his personality. We see the laughing, rejoicing child who, while he picks the berries from the edge of the precipice, is not aware that he must fall down if the hero does not snatch him back at the last moment. Of course, we feel the child's joy with him. Otherwise, we should not even understand his behaviour, but we feel more strongly the fear and the horror of which the child himself does not know anything. The photoplaywrights have, so far, hardly ventured to project this second class of emotion, which the spectator superadds to the events, into the show on the screen. Only tentative suggestions can be found. The enthusiasm or the disapproval or indignation of the spectator is sometimes released in the lights and shades and in the setting of the landscape. There are still rich possibilities along this line. The photoplay has hardly come to its own with regard to these secondary emotions. Here, it has not emancipated itself sufficiently from the model of the stage. Those emotions arise, of course, in the audience of a theater too, but the dramatic stage cannot embody them. In the opera, the orchestra may symbolize them. For the photoplay, which is not bound to the physical succession of events but gives us only the pictorial reflection, there is an unlimited field for the expression of these attitudes in ourselves.

But the wide expansion of this field and of the whole manifoldness of emotional possibilities in the moving pictures is not sufficiently characterized as long as we think only of the optical representation in the actual outer world. The camera men of the moving pictures have photographed the happenings of the world and all its wonders, have gone to the bottom of the sea and up to the clouds; they have surprised the beasts in the jungles and in the Arctic ice; they have dwelt with the lowest races and have captured the greatest men of our time; and they are always haunted by the fear that the supply of new sensations may be exhausted. Curiously enough, they have so far ignored the fact that an inexhaustible wealth of new impressions is at their disposal, which has hardly been touched as yet. There is a material and a formal side to the pictures which we see in their rapid succession. The material side is controlled by the content of what is shown to us. But the formal side depends upon the outer conditions under which this content is exhibited. Even with ordinary photographs we are accustomed to discriminate between those in which every detail is very sharp and others, often much more artistic, in which everything looks somewhat misty and blurring and in which sharp outlines are avoided. We have this formal aspect, of course, still more prominently if we see the same landscape or the same person painted by a dozen different artists. Each one has his own style. Or, to point to another elementary factor, the same series of moving pictures may be given to us with a very slow or with a rapid turning of the crank. It is the same street scene, and yet in the one case everyone on the street seems leisurely to saunter along, while in the other case there is a general rush and hurry. Nothing is changed but the temporal form; and in going over from the sharp image to the blurring one, nothing is changed but a certain spatial form, the content remains the same.

As soon as we give any interest to this formal aspect of the presentation, we must recognize that the photoplaywright has here possibilities to which nothing corresponds in the world of the stage. Take the case that we want to produce an effect of trembling. We might use the pictures as the camera has taken them, sixteen in a second. But in reproducing them on the screen we change their order. After giving the first four pictures we go back to picture 3, then give 4, 5, 6, and return to 5, then 6, 7, 8, and go back to 7, and so on.

Any other rhythm, of course, is equally possible. The effect is one which never occurs in nature and which could not be produced on the stage. The events for a moment go backward. A certain vibration goes through the world like the tremolo of the orchestra. Or we demand from our camera a still more complex service. We put the camera itself on a slightly rocking support, and then every point must move in strange curves and every motion takes an uncanny whirling character. The content still remains the same as under normal conditions, but the changes in the formal presentation give to the mind of the spectator unusual sensations which produce a new shading of the emotional background.

Of course, impressions which come to our eye at first awaken only sensations, and a sensation is not an emotion. But it is well known that, in the view of modern physiological psychology, our consciousness of the emotion itself is shaped and marked by the sensations which arise from our bodily organs. As soon as such abnormal visual impressions stream into our consciousness, our whole background of fusing bodily sensations becomes altered, and new emotions seem to take hold of us. If we see on the screen a man hypnotized in the doctor's office, the patient himself may lie there with closed eyes, nothing in his features expressing his emotional setting and nothing radiating to us. But if now only the doctor and the patient remain unchanged and steady, while everything in the whole room begins at first to tremble and then to wave and to change its form more and more rapidly so that a feeling of dizziness comes over us and an uncanny, ghastly unnaturalness overcomes the whole surrounding of the hypnotized person, we ourselves become seized by the strange emotion. It is not worth while to go into further illustrations here, as this possibility of the camera work still belongs entirely to the future. It could not be otherwise as we remember that the whole moving picture play arose from the slavish imitation of the drama and began only slowly to find its own artistic methods. But there is no doubt that the formal changes of the pictorial presentation will be legion as soon as the photoartists give their attention to this neglected aspect.

The value of these formal changes for the expression of the emotions may become remarkable. The characteristic features of many an attitude and feeling which cannot be expressed without words today will then be aroused in the mind of the spectator through the subtle art of the camera.

Part II: The Aesthetics of the Photoplay

Chapter 7: **The Purpose of Art**

We have analyzed the mental functions which are most powerful in the audience of the photoplay. We studied the mere act of perceiving the pictures on the screen, of perceiving their apparently plastic character, their depth, and their apparent movements. We turned then to those psychical acts by which we respond to the perceived impressions. In the foreground stood the act of attention, but then we followed the play of associations, of memory, of imagination, of suggestion, and, most important of all, we traced the distribution of interest. Finally, we spoke of the feelings and emotions with which we accompany the play. Certainly, all this does not exhaust the mental reactions which arise in our mind when we witness a drama of the film. We have not spoken, for instance, of the action which the plot of the story or its social background may start in our soul. The suffering of the poor, the injustice by which the weak may be forced into the path of crime, and a hundred other social motives may be impressed on us by the photoplay; thoughts about human society, about laws and reforms, about human differences and human fates, may fill our mind. Yet this is not one of the characteristic functions of the moving pictures. It is a side effect which may set in, just as it may result from reading the newspapers or from hearing of practical affairs in life. But in all our discussions, we have also left out another mental process, namely, aesthetic emotion. We did speak about the emotions which the plot of the play stirs up. We discussed the feelings in which we sympathize with the characters of the scene, in which we share their suffering and their joy;

and we also spoke about that other group of emotions by which we take a mental attitude toward the behaviour of the persons in the play. But there is surely a third group of feelings and emotions which we have not yet considered, namely, those of our joy in the play, our aesthetic satisfaction or dissatisfaction. We have omitted them intentionally, because the study of this group of feelings involves a discussion of the aesthetic process as such, and we have left all the aesthetic problems for this second part of our investigation.

If we disregard this pleasure or displeasure in the beauty of the photoplay and reflect only on the processes of perception, attention, interest, memory, imagination, suggestion, and emotion which we have analyzed, we see that we everywhere come to the same result. One general principle seemed to control the whole mental mechanism of the spectator, or rather the relation between the mental mechanism and the pictures on the screen. We recognized that, in every case, the objective world of outer events had been shaped and molded until it became adjusted to the subjective movements of the mind. The mind develops memory ideas and imaginative ideas; in the moving pictures they become reality. The mind concentrates itself on a special detail in its act of attention; and in the close-up of the moving pictures this inner state is objectified. The mind is filled with emotions; and by means of the camera the whole scenery echoes them. Even in the most objective factor of the mind, the perception, we find this peculiar oscillation. We perceive the movement; and yet we perceive it as something which has not its independent character as an outer world process, because our mind has built it up from single pictures rapidly following one another. We perceive things in their plastic depth; and yet again the depth is not that of the outer world. We are aware of its unreality and of the pictorial flatness of the impressions.

In every one of these features, the contrast to the mental impressions from the real stage is obvious. There in the theater, we know at every moment that we see real plastic men before us, that they are really in motion when they walk and talk and that, on the other hand, it is our own doing and not a part of the play when our attention turns to this or that detail, when our memory brings back events of the past, when our imagination surrounds them with fancies and emotions. And here, it seems, we have a definite starting point for an aesthetic comparison. If we raise the unavoidable question—how does the photoplay compare with the drama?—we seem to have sufficient material on hand to form an aesthetic judgment. The verdict, it appears, can hardly be doubtful. Must we not say art is imitation of nature? The drama can show us on the stage a true imitation of real life. The scenes proceed just as they would happen anywhere in the outer world. Men of flesh and blood with really plastic bodies stand before us. They move like any moving body in our surroundings. Moreover those happenings on the stage, just like the events in life, are independent of our subjective attention and memory and imagination. They go their objective course. Thus, the theater comes so near to its purpose of imitating the world of men that the comparison with the photoplay suggests almost a disastrous failure of the art of the film. The color of the world has disappeared, the persons are dumb, no sound reaches our ear. The depth of the scene appears unreal, the motion has lost its natural character. Worst of all, the objective course of events is falsified; our own attention and memory and imagination have shifted and remodeled the events until they look as nature could never show them. What we really see can hardly be called any longer an imitation of the world, such as the theater gives us.

When the graphophone repeats a Beethoven symphony, the voluminousness of the orchestra is reduced to a thin feeble surface sound, and no one would accept this product of the disk and the diaphragm as a full substitute for the performance of the real orchestra. But, after all, every instrument is actually represented, and we can still discriminate the violins and the celli and the flutes in exactly the same order and tonal and rhythmic relation in which they appear in the original. The graphophone music appears, therefore, much better fitted for replacing the orchestra than the moving pictures are to be a substitute for the theater. There, all the essential elements seem conserved; here, just the essentials seem to be lost and the aim of the drama to imitate life with the greatest possible reality seems hopelessly beyond the flat, colorless pictures of the photoplay. Still more might we say that the plaster of Paris cast is a fair substitute for the marble statue. It shares with the beautiful marble work the same form and imitates the body of the living man just as well as the marble statue. Moreover, this product of the mechanical process has the same white color which the original work of the sculptor possesses. Hence, we must acknowledge it as a fair approach to the plastic work of art. In the same way, the chromo print gives the essentials of the oil painting. Everywhere, the technical process has secured a reproduction of the work of art which sounds or looks almost like the work of the great artist, and only the technique of the moving pictures, which so clearly tries to reproduce the theater performance, stands so utterly far behind the art of the actor. Is not an aesthetic judgment of rejection demanded by good taste and sober criticism? We may tolerate the photoplay because, by the inexpensive technical method which allows an unlimited multiplication of the performances, it brings at least a shadow of the theater to the masses who cannot afford to see real actors. But the cultivated mind might better enjoy plaster of Paris casts and chromo prints and graphophone music than the moving pictures with their complete failure to give us the essentials of the real stage.

We have heard this message, or if it was not expressed in clear words it surely lingered for a long while in the minds of all those who had a serious relation to art. It probably still prevails today among many, even if they appreciate the more ambitious efforts of the photoplaywrights in the most recent years. The philanthropic pleasure in the furnishing of cheap entertainment and the recognition that a certain advance has recently been made seem to alleviate the aesthetic situation, but the core of public opinion remains the same; the moving pictures are no real art.

And yet all this arguing and all this hasty settling of a most complex problem is fundamentally wrong. It is based on entirely mistaken ideas concerning the aims and purposes of art. If those errors were given up and if the right understanding of the moving pictures were to take hold of the community, nobody would doubt that the chromo print and the graphophone and the plaster cast are indeed nothing but inexpensive substitutes for art with many essential artistic elements left out, and therefore ultimately unsatisfactory to a truly artistic taste. But everybody would recognize at the same time that the relation of the photoplay to the theater is a completely different one and that the difference counts entirely in favor of the moving pictures. *They are not and ought never to be imitations of the theater. They can never give the aesthetic values of the theater; but no more can the theater give the aesthetic values of the photoplay.* With the rise of the moving pictures has come an entirely new independent art which must develop its own life conditions. The moving pictures would indeed be a complete failure if that popular theory of art which we suggested were right. But that theory is wrong from beginning to end, and it must not obstruct the way to a better insight which recognizes that the stage and the screen are as fundamentally different as sculpture and painting, or as lyrics and music. *The drama and the photoplay are two coordinated arts, each perfectly valuable in itself.* The one cannot replace the other, and the shortcomings of the one as against the other reflect only the fact that the one has a history of fifteen years while the other has one of five thousand. This is the thesis which we want to prove, and the first step to it must be to ask: what is the aim of art if not the imitation of reality?

But can the claim that art imitates nature, or rather that imitation is the essence of art, be upheld if we seriously look over the field of artistic creations? Would it not involve the expectation that the artistic value would be the greater, the more the ideal of imitation is approached? A perfect imitation which looks exactly like the original would give us the highest art. Yet every page in the history of art tells us the opposite. We admire the marble statue, and we despise as inartistic the colored wax figures. There is no difficulty in producing colored wax figures which look so completely like real persons that the visitor at an exhibit may easily be deceived and may ask information from the wax man leaning over the railing. On the other hand, what a tremendous distance between reality and the marble statue with its uniform white surface! It could never deceive us and as an imitation it would certainly be a failure. Is it different with a painting? Here the color may be quite similar to the original, but unlike the marble it has lost its depth and shows us nature on a flat surface. Again, we could never be deceived, and it is not the painter's ambition to make us believe for a moment that reality is before us. Moreover, neither the sculptor nor the painter gives us less valuable work when they offer us a bust or a painted head only instead of the whole figure, and yet, we have never seen in reality a human body ending at the chest. We admire a fine etching hardly less than a painting. Here we have neither the plastic effect of the sculpture nor the color of the painting. The essential features of the real model are left out. As an imitation, it would fail disastrously. What is imitated in a lyric poem? Through more than two thousand years, we have appreciated the works of the great dramatists who had their personages speak in the rhythms of metrical language. Every iambic verse is a deviation from reality. If they had tried to imitate nature, *Antigone* and *Hamlet* would have spoken the prose of daily life. Does a beautiful arch or dome or tower of a building imitate any part of reality? Is its architectural value dependent upon the similarity to nature? Or does the melody or harmony in music offer an imitation of the surrounding world?

Wherever we examine without prejudice the mental effects of true works of art in literature or music, in painting or sculpture, in decorative arts or architecture, we find that the central aesthetic value is directly opposed to the spirit of imitation. A work of art may and must start from something which awakens in us the interests of reality and which contains traits of reality, and to that extent it cannot avoid some imitation. But *it becomes art just in so far as it overcomes reality, stops imitating and leaves the imitated reality behind it.* It is artistic just in so far as it does not imitate reality but changes the world, selects from it special features for new purposes, remodels the world, and is, through this, truly creative. To imitate the world is a mechanical process; to transform the world so that it becomes a thing of beauty is the purpose of art. The highest art may be furthest removed from reality.

We have not even the right to say that this process of selection from reality means that we keep the beautiful elements of it and simply omit and eliminate the ugly ones. This, again, is not in the least characteristic of art, however often the popular mind may couple this superficial idea with that other one, that art consists of imitation. It is not true that the aesthetic value depends upon the beauty of the selected material. The men and women whom Rembrandt painted were not beautiful persons. The ugliest woman may be the subject of a most beautiful painting. The so-called beautiful landscape may, of course, be material for a beautiful landscape painting, but the chances are great that such a pretty vista will attract the dilettante and not the real artist, who knows that the true value of his painting is independent of the prettiness of the model. He knows that a muddy country road, or a dirty city street, or a trivial little pond may be the material for immortal pictures. He who writes literature does not select scenes of life which are beautiful in themselves, scenes which we would have liked to live through, full of radiant happiness and joy; he does not eliminate from his picture of life that which is disturbing to the peace of the soul, repellant and ugly and immoral. On the contrary, all the great works of literature have shown us dark shades of life beside the light ones. They have spoken of unhappiness and pain as often as of joy. We have suffered with our poets, and in so far as the musical composer expresses the emotions of life, the great symphonies have been full of pathos and tragedy. True art has always been selection, but never selection of the beautiful elements in outer reality.

But if the aesthetic value is independent of the imitative approach to reality and independent of the elimination of unpleasant elements or of the collection and addition of pleasant traits, what does the artist really select and combine in his creation? How does he shape the world? How does nature look when it has been remolded by the artistic temperament and imagination? What is left of the real landscape when the engraver's needle has sketched it? What is left of the tragic events in real life when the lyric poet has reshaped them in a few rhymed stanzas? Perhaps we may bring the characteristic features of the process most easily to recognition if we contrast them with another kind of reshaping process. The same landscape which the artist sketches, the same historic events which the lyric poet interprets in his verses, may be grasped by the human mind in a wholly different way. We need only think of the scientific work of the scholar. He, too, may have the greatest interest in the landscape which the engraver has rendered: the tree on the edge of the rock, torn by the storm, and, at the foot of the cliff, the sea with its whitecapped waves. He, too, is absorbed by the tragic death of a Lincoln. But what is the scholar's attitude? Is it his aim to reproduce the landscape or the historic event? Certainly not. The meaning of science and scholarship and of knowledge in general would be completely misunderstood if their aim were thought to be simply the repeating of the special facts in reality. The scientist tries to explain the facts, and even his description is meant to serve his explanation. He turns to that tree on the cliff with the interest of studying its anatomical structure. He examines with a microscope the cells of those tissues in the branches and leaves in order that he may explain the growth of the tree and its development from the germ. The storm which whips its branches is to him a physical process for which he seeks the causes, far removed. The sea is to him a substance which he resolves in his laboratory into its chemical elements and which he explains by tracing the geological changes on the surface of the earth.

In short, the scientist is not interested in that particular object only, but in its connections with the total universe. He explains the event by a reference to general laws which are effective everywhere. Every single growth and movement is linked by him with the endless chain of causes and effects. He surely reshapes the experience in connecting every single impression with the totality of events, in finding the general in the particular, in transforming the given facts into the scientific scheme of an atomistic universe. It is not different from the historical event. To the scholarly historian, the death of Lincoln is meaningless if it is not seen in its relation to and connection with the whole history of the Civil War, and if this again is not understood as the result of the total development of the United States. And who can understand the growth of the United States, unless the whole of modern history is seen as a background and unless the ideas of state philosophy which have built up the American democracy are grasped in their connection with the whole story of European political thought in preceding centuries? The scholar may turn to natural or to social events, to waves or trees or men: every process and action in the world gains interest for him only by being connected with other things and events. Every point which he marks is the nodal point for numberless relations. To grasp a fact in the sense of scholarly knowledge means to see it in all its connections, and the work of the scholar is not simply to hold the fact as he becomes aware of it, but to trace the connections and to supplement them by his thought until a completed system of interrelated facts in science or in history is established.

Now we are better prepared to recognize the characteristic function of the artist. He is doing exactly the opposite of what the scholar is aiming at. Both are changing and remolding the given thing or event in the interest of their ideal aims. But the ideal aim of beauty and art is in complete contrast to the ideal aim of scholarly knowledge. The scholar, we see, establishes connections by which the special thing loses all character of separateness. He binds it to all the remainder of the physical and social universe. The artist, on the contrary, cuts off every possible connection. He puts his landscape into a frame, so that every possible link with the surrounding world is severed. He places his statue on a pedestal, so that it cannot possibly step into the room around it. He makes his persons speak in verse, so that they cannot possibly be connected with the intercourse of the day. He tells his story, so that nothing can happen after the last chapter. *The work of art shows us the things and events perfectly complete in themselves, freed from all connections which lead beyond their own limits, that is, in perfect isolation.*

Both the truth which the scholar discovers and the beauty which the artist creates are valuable, but it is now clear that the value in both cases lies not in the mere repetition of the offerings of reality. There is no reason whatever for appreciating a mere imitation or repetition of that which exists in the world. Neither the scholar nor the artist could do better than nature or history. The value in both cases lies just in the deviation from reality in the service of human desires and ideals. The desire and ideal of the scholar is to give us an interconnected world in which we understand everything by its being linked with everything else, and the desire and ideal of the artist in every possible art is to give us things which are freed from the connection of the world and which stand before us complete in themselves. The things of the outer world have thousandfold ties with nature and history. An object becomes beautiful when it is delivered from these ties, and in order to secure this result we must take it away from the background of reality and reproduce it in such a form that it is unmistakably different from the real things which are enchained by the causes and effects of nature.

Why does this satisfy us? Why is it valuable to have a part of nature or life liberated from all connection with the world? Why does it make us happy to see anything in its perfect isolation, an isolation which real life seldom offers and which only art can give in complete perfection? The motives which lead us to value the product of the scholar are easily recognized. He aims toward connection. He reshapes the world until it appears connected, because that helps us to foresee the effects of every event and teaches us to master nature so that we can use it for our practical achievements. But why do we appreciate no less the opposite work which the artist is doing? Might we not answer that this enjoyment of the artistic work results from the fact that only in contact with an isolated experience can we feel perfectly happy? Whatever we meet in life or nature awakes in us desires, impulses to action, suggestions and questions which must be answered. Life is a continuous striving. Nothing is an end in itself, and, therefore, nothing is a source of complete rest. Everything is a stimulus to new wishes, a source of new uneasiness which longs for new satisfaction in the next and again the next thing. Life pushes us forward. Yet sometimes a touch of nature comes to us; we are stirred by a thrill of life which awakens plenty of impulses but which offers satisfaction to all these impulses in itself. It does not lead beyond itself, but contains in its own midst everything which answers the questions, which brings the desires to rest.

Wherever we meet such an offering of nature, we call it beautiful. We speak of the beautiful landscape, of the beautiful face. And wherever we meet it in life, we speak of love, of friendship, of peace, of harmony. The word harmony may even cover both nature and life. Wherever it happens that every line and every curve and every color and every movement in the landscape is so harmonious with all the others that every suggestion which one stirs up is satisfied by another, there it is perfect, and we are completely happy in it. In the life relations of love and friendship and peace, there is again this complete harmony of thought and feeling and will, in which every desire is satisfied. If our own mind is in such flawless harmony, we feel the true happiness which crowns our life. Such harmony, in which every part is the complete fulfillment of that which the other parts demand, when nothing is suggested which is not fulfilled in the midst of the same experience, where nothing points beyond and everything is complete in the offering itself, must be a source of inexhaustible happiness. To remold nature and life so that it offers such complete harmony in itself that it does not point beyond its own limits but is an ultimate unity through the harmony of its parts, this is the aim of the isolation which the artist alone achieves. That restful happiness which the beautiful landscape or the harmonious life relation can furnish us in blessed instants of our struggling life is secured as a joy forever when the painter or the sculptor, the dramatist or the poet, the composer or the photoplaywright, recomposes nature and life and shows us a unity which does not lead beyond itself but is in itself perfectly harmonious.

Chapter 8: **The Means of the Various Arts**

We have sought the aim which underlies all artistic creation and were led in this search to paths which seem far away from our special problem, the art of the photoplay. Yet we have steadily come nearer to it. We had to go the longer way because there can be no other method to reach a decision concerning the aesthetic value and significance of the photoplay. We must clearly see what art in general aims at if we want to recognize the relative standing of the film art and the art of the theater. If we superficially accept the popular idea that the value of the photoplay is to be measured by the nearness with which it approaches the standards of the real theater and that the task of the theater is to imitate life as closely as possible, the aesthetic condemnation of the photoplay is necessary. The pictures on the screen then stand far behind the actual playing on the stage in every respect. But if we find that the aim of art, including the dramatic art, is not to imitate life but to reset it in a way which is totally different from reality, then an entirely new perspective is opened. The dramatic way may then be only one of the artistic possibilities. The kinematoscopic way may be another, which may have entirely different methods, and yet may be just as valuable and aesthetically pure as the art of the theater. The drama and the photoplay may serve the purpose of art with equal sincerity and perfection and may reach the same goal with sharply contrasting means. Our next step, which brings us directly to the threshold of the photoplayhouse, is, accordingly, to study the difference of the various methods which the different arts use for their common purpose. What characterizes a particular art as such? When we have recognized the special traits of the traditional arts, we shall be better prepared to ask whether the methods of the photoplay do not characterize this film creation also as a full-fledged art, coordinated with the older forms of beauty.

We saw that the aim of every art is to isolate some object of experience in nature or social life in such a way that it becomes complete in itself, and satisfies by itself every demand which it awakens. If every desire which it stimulates is completely fulfilled by its own parts, that is, if it is a complete harmony, we, the spectators, the listeners, the readers, are perfectly satisfied, and this complete satisfaction is the characteristic aesthetic joy. The first demand which is involved in this characterization of art is that the offering of the artist shall really awaken interests, as only a constant stirring up of desires together with their constant fulfillment keeps the flame of aesthetic enjoyment alive. When nothing stirs us, when nothing interests us, we are in a state of indifference outside the realm of art. This also separates the aesthetic pleasure from the ordinary selfish pleasures of life. They are based on the satisfaction of desires, too, but a kind of satisfaction through which the desire itself disappears. The pleasure in a meal, to be sure, can have its aesthetic side, as often the harmony of the tastes and odors and sights of a rich feast may be brought to a certain artistic perfection. But mere pleasure in eating has no aesthetic value, as the object is destroyed by the partaking and not only the cake disappears but also our desire for the cake, when the desire is fulfilled and we are satiated. The work of art aims to keep both the demand and its fulfillment forever awake.

But then this stirring up of interests demands more than anything else a careful selection of those features in reality which ought to be admitted into the work of art. A thousand traits of the landscape are trivial and insignificant and most of what happens in the social life around us, even where a great action is going on, is in itself commonplace and dull and without consequences for the event which stirs us. The very first requirement for the artistic creation is, therefore, the elimination of the indifferent, the selection of those features of the complex offering of nature or social life which tell the real story, which express the true emotional values, and which suggest the interest for everything which is involved in this particular episode of the world. But this leads on to the natural consequence, that the artist must not only select the important traits, but must artificially heighten their power and increase their strength. We spoke of the landscape with the tree on the rock and the roaring surf, and we saw how the scientist studies its smallest elements, the cells of the tree, the molecules of the seawater and of the rock. How differently does the artist proceed! He does not care even for the single leaves which the photographer might reproduce. If a painter renders such a landscape with his masterly brush, he gives us only the leading movements of those branches which the storm tears, and the great swing in the curve of the wave. But those forceful lines of the billows, those sharp contours of the rock, contain everything which expresses their spirit.

It is not different with the author who writes a historical novel or drama. Every man's life is crowded with the trivialities of the day. The scholarly historian may have to look into them; the artist selects those events in his hero's life which truly express his personality and which are fit to sustain the significant plot. The more he brings those few elements out of the many into sharp relief, the more he stimulates our interest and makes us really feel with the persons of his novel or drama. The sculptor even selects one single position. He cannot, like the painter, give us any background, he cannot make his hero move as on the theater stage. The marble statue makes the one position of the hero everlasting, but this is so selected that all the chance aspects and fleeting gestures of the real man appear insignificant compared with the one most expressive and most characteristic position which is chosen.

However far this selection of the essential traits removes the artistic creation from the mere imitative reproduction of the world, a much greater distance from reality results from a second need if the work is to fulfill the purposes of art. We saw that we have art only when the work is isolated, that is, when it fulfills every demand in itself and does not point beyond itself. This can be done only if it is sharply set off from the sphere of our practical interests. Whatever enters into our practical sphere links itself with our impulses to real action, and the action would involve a change, an intrusion, an influence from without. As long as we have the desire to change anything, the work is not complete in itself. The relation of the work to us as persons must not enter into our awareness of it at all. As soon as it does, that complete restfulness of the aesthetic enjoyment is lost. Then the object becomes simply a part of our practical surroundings. The fundamental condition of art, therefore, is that we shall be distinctly conscious of the unreality of the artistic production, and that means that it must be absolutely separated from the real things and men, that it must be isolated and kept in its own sphere. As soon as a work of art tempts us to take it as a piece of reality, it has been dragged into the sphere of our practical action, which means our desire to put ourselves into connection with it. Its completeness in itself is lost, and its value for our aesthetic enjoyment has faded away.

Now, we understand why it is necessary that each art should have its particular method for fundamentally changing reality. Now, we recognize that it is by no means a weakness of sculpture that the marble statue has not the colors of life but a whiteness unlike any human being. Nor does it appear a deficiency in the painting or the drawing that it can offer two dimensions only and has no means to show us the depth of real nature. Now, we grasp why the poet expresses his feelings and thoughts in the entirely unnatural language of rhythms and rhymes. Now, we see why every work of art has its frame or its base or its stage. Everything serves that central purpose, the separation of the offered experience from the background of our real life. When we have a painted garden before us, we do not want to pick the flowers from the beds and break the fruit from the branches. The flatness of the picture tells us that this is no reality, in spite of the fact that the size of the painting may not be different from that of the windowpane through which we see a real garden. We have no thought of bringing a chair or a warm coat for the woman in marble. The work which the sculptor created stands before us in a space into which we cannot enter, and because it is entirely removed from the reality toward which our actions are directed, we become aesthetic spectators only. The smile of the marble girl wins us as if it came from a living one, but we do not respond to her welcome. Just as she appears in her marble form, she is complete in herself without any relation to us or to anyone else. The very difference from reality has given her that self-sustained perfect life.

If we read in a police report about burglaries, we may lock our house more securely; if we read about a flood, we may send our mite; if we read about an elopement, we may try to find out what happened later. But if we read about all these in a short story, we have aesthetic enjoyment only if the author somehow makes it perfectly clear to us by the form of the description that this burglary and flood and elopement do not belong to our real surroundings and exist only in the world of imagination. The extreme case comes to us in the theater performance. We see there real human beings a few feet from us; we see in the melodrama how the villain approaches his victim from behind with a dagger; we feel indignation and anger; and yet we have not the slightest desire to jump up on the stage and stay his arm. The artificial setting of the stage, the lighted proscenium before the dark house, have removed the whole action from the world which is connected with our own deeds. The consciousness of unreality, which the theater has forced on us, is the condition for our dramatic interest in the events presented. If we were really deceived and only for a moment took the stage quarrel and stage crime to be real, we would at once be removed from the height of aesthetic joy to the level of common experience.

We must take one step more. We need not only the complete separation from reality by the changed forms of experience, but we must demand also that this unreal thing or event shall be complete in itself. The artist, therefore, must do whatever is needed to satisfy the demands which any part awakens. If one line in the painting suggests a certain mood and movement, the other lines must take it up, and the colors must sympathize with it, and they all must agree with the pictured content. The tension which one scene in the drama awakens must be relieved by another. Nothing must remain unexplained and nothing unfinished. We do not want to know what is going on behind the hills of the landscape painting or what the couple in the comedy will do after the engagement in the last act. On the other hand, if the artist adds elements which are in harmony with the demands of the other parts, they are aesthetically valuable, however much they may differ from the actual happenings in the outer world. In the painting, the mermaid may have her tail, and the sculptured child may have his angel wings, and fairies may appear on the stage. In short, every demand which is made by the purpose of true art removes us from reality and is contrary to the superficial claim that art ought to rest on skillful imitation. The true victory of art lies in the overcoming of the real appearance and every art is genuine which fulfills this aesthetic desire for history or for nature, in its own way.

The number of ways cannot be determined beforehand. By the study of painting and etching and drawing merely, we could not foresee that there is also possible an art like sculpture, and by studying epic and lyric poetry, we could not construct beforehand the forms of the drama. The genius of mankind had to discover ever new forms in which the interest in reality is conserved and yet the things and events are so completely changed that they are separated from all possible reality, isolated from all connections and made complete in themselves. We have not yet spoken about the one art which gives us this perfect satisfaction in the isolated material, satisfies every demand which it awakens, and yet which is further removed from the reality we know than any other artistic creation, music. Those tones with which the composer builds up his melodies and harmonies are not parts of the world in which we live at all. None of our actions in practical life is related to tones from musical instruments, and yet the tones of a symphony may arouse in us the deepest emotions, the most solemn feelings, and the most joyful ones. They are symbols of our world which bring with them its sadness and its happiness. We feel the rhythm of the tones, fugitive, light and joyful, or quiet, heavy and sustained, and they impress us as energies which awaken our own impulses, our own tensions and relaxations.

We enter into the play of those tones which, with their intervals and their instrumental tone color, appear like a wonderful mosaic of agreements and disagreements. Yet each disagreement resolves itself into a new agreement. Those tones seek one another. They have life of their own, complete in itself. We do not want to change it. Our mind simply echoes their desires and their satisfaction. We feel with them and are happy in their ultimate agreement without which no musical melody would be beautiful. Bound by the inner law which is proclaimed by the first tones, every coming tone is prepared. The whole tone movement points toward the next one. It is a world of inner self-agreement like that of the colors in a painting, of the curves in a work of sculpture, like the rhythms and rhymes in a stanza. But beyond the mere self-agreement of the tones and rhythms as such, the musical piece as a whole unveils to us a world of emotion. Music does not depict the physical nature which fine arts bring to us, nor the social world which literature embraces, but the inner world with its abundance of feelings and excitements. It isolates our inner experience and, within its limits, brings it to that perfect self-agreement which is the characteristic of every art.

We might easily trace further the various means by which each particular art overcomes the chaos of the world and renders a part of it in a perfectly isolated form in which all elements are in mutual agreement. We might develop out of this fundamental demand of art all the special forms which are characteristic in its various fields. We might also turn to the applied arts, to architecture, to arts and crafts, and so on, and see how new rules must arise from the combination of purely artistic demands and those of practical utility. But this would lead us too far into aesthetic theory, while our aim is to push forward toward the problem of the photoplay. Of painting, of drama, and of music, we had to speak because with them the photoplay does share certain important conditions and, accordingly, certain essential forms of rendering the world. Each element of the photoplay is a picture, flat like that which the painter creates, and the pictorial character is fundamental for the art of the film. But, surely, the photoplay shares many conditions with the drama on the stage. The presentation of conflicting action among men in dramatic scenes is the content, on the stage as on the screen. Our chief claim, however, was that we falsify the meaning of the photoplay if we simply subordinate it to the aesthetic conditions of the drama. It is different from mere pictures, and it is different from the drama, too, however much relation it has to both. But we come nearer to the understanding of its true position in the aesthetic world if we think at the same time of that other art upon which we touched, the art of the musical tones. They have overcome the outer world and the social world entirely, they unfold our inner life, our mental play, with its feelings and emotions, its memories and fancies, in a material which seems exempt from the laws of the world of substance and material, tones which are fluttering and fleeting like our own mental states. Of course, a photoplay is not a piece of music. Its material is not sound but light. But the photoplay is not music in the same sense in which it is not drama and not pictures. It shares something with all of them. It stands somewhere among and apart from them, and just for this reason it is an art of a particular type which must be understood through its own conditions and for which its own aesthetic rules must be traced, instead of drawing them simply from the rules of the theater.

Chapter 9: **The Means of the Photoplay**

We have now reached the point at which we can knot together all our threads, the psychological and the aesthetic ones. If we do so, we come to the true thesis of this whole book. Our aesthetic discussion showed us that it is the aim of art to isolate a significant part of our experience in such a way that it is separate from our practical life and is in complete agreement within itself. Our aesthetic satisfaction results from this inner agreement and harmony, but, in order that we may feel such agreement of the parts, we must enter with our own impulses into the will of every element, into the meaning of every line and color and form, every word and tone and note. Only if everything is full of such inner movement can we really enjoy the harmonious cooperation of the parts. The means of the various arts, we saw, are the forms and methods by which this aim is fulfilled. They must be different for every material. Moreover, the same material may allow very different methods of isolation and elimination of the insignificant and reinforcement of that which contributes to the harmony. If we ask now what are the characteristic means by which the photoplay succeeds in overcoming reality, in isolating a significant dramatic story, and in presenting it so that we enter into it and yet keep it away from our practical life and enjoy the harmony of the parts, we must remember all the results to which our psychological discussion in the first part of the book has led us.

We recognized there that the photoplay, incomparable in this respect with the drama, gave us a view of dramatic events which was completely shaped by the inner movements of the mind. To be sure, the events in the photoplay happen in the real space with its depth. But the spectator feels that they are not presented in the three dimensions of the outer world, that they are flat pictures which only the mind molds into plastic things. Again, the events are seen in continuous movement, and yet the pictures break up the movement into a rapid succession of instantaneous impressions. We do not see the objective reality, but a product of our own mind which binds the pictures together. But much stronger differences came to light when we turned to the processes of attention, of memory, of imagination, of suggestion, of division of interest, and of emotion. The attention turns to detailed points in the outer world and ignores everything else; the photoplay is doing exactly this when, in the close-up, a detail is enlarged and everything else disappears. Memory breaks into present events by bringing up pictures of the past; the photoplay is doing this by its frequent cut-backs when pictures of events long past flit between those of the present. The imagination anticipates the future or overcomes reality by fancies and dreams, the photoplay is doing all this more richly than any chance imagination would succeed in doing. But chiefly, through our division of interest, our mind is drawn hither and thither. We think of events which run parallel in different places. The photoplay can show in intertwined scenes everything which our mind embraces. Events in three or four or five regions of the world can be woven together into one complex action. Finally, we saw that every shade of feeling and emotion which fills the spectator's mind can mold the scenes in the photoplay until they appear the embodiment of our feelings. In every one of these aspects, the photoplay succeeds in doing what the drama of the theater does not attempt.

If this is the outcome of aesthetic analysis on the one side, of psychological research on the other, we need only combine the results of both into a unified principle: *the photoplay tells us the human story by overcoming the forms of the outer world, namely, space, time, and causality, and by adjusting the events to the forms of the inner world, namely, attention, memory, imagination, and emotion.*

We shall gain our orientation most directly if once more, under this point of view, we compare the photoplay with the performance on the theater stage. We shall not enter into a discussion of the character of the regular theater and its drama. We take this for granted. Everybody knows that highest art form which the Greeks created and which, from Greece, has spread over Asia, Europe, and America. In tragedy and in comedy from ancient times to Ibsen, Rostand, Hauptmann, and Shaw, we recognize one common purpose and one common form for which no further commentary is needed. How does the photoplay differ from a theater performance? We insisted that every work of art must be somehow separated from our sphere of practical interests. The theater is no exception. The structure of the theater itself, the framelike form of the stage, the difference of light between stage and house, the stage setting and costuming, all inhibit in the audience the possibility of taking the action on the stage to be real life. Stage managers have sometimes tried the experiment of reducing those differences, for instance, keeping the audience also in a fully lighted hall, and they always had to discover how much the dramatic effect was reduced because the feeling of distance from reality was weakened. The photoplay and the theater in this respect are evidently alike. The screen, too, suggests from the very start the complete unreality of the events.

But each further step leads us to remarkable differences between the stage play and the film play. In every respect, the film play is further away from the physical reality than the drama, and in every respect, this greater distance from the physical world brings it nearer to the mental world. The stage shows us living men. It is not the real Romeo and not the real Juliet, and yet the actor and the actress have the ringing voices of true people, breathe like them, have living colors like them, and fill physical space like them. What is left in the photoplay? The voice has been stilled: the photoplay is a dumb show. Yet we must not forget that this alone is a step away from reality which has often been taken in the midst of the dramatic world. Whoever knows the history of the theater is aware of the tremendous role which the pantomime has played in the development of mankind. From the old half-religious pantomimic and suggestive dances out of which the beginnings of the real drama grew to the fully religious pantomimes of medieval ages, and further on, to many silent mimic elements in modern performances, we find a continuity of conventions which make the pantomime almost the real background of all dramatic development.

We know how popular the pantomimes were among the Greeks, and how they stood in the foreground in the imperial period of Rome. Old Rome cherished the mimic clowns, but still more the tragic pantomimics. "Their very nod speaks, their hands talk and their fingers have a voice." After the fall of the Roman empire, the church used the pantomime for the portrayal of sacred history, and later centuries enjoyed very unsacred histories in the pantomimes of their ballets. Even complex artistic tragedies without words have triumphed on our present-day stage. *L'Enfant Prodigue* which came from Paris, *Sumurun* which came from Berlin, *Petroushka* which came from Petrograd, conquered the American stage; and surely the loss of speech, while it increased the remoteness from reality, by no means destroyed the continuous consciousness of the bodily existence of the actors.

Moreover, the student of a modern pantomime cannot overlook a characteristic difference between the speechless performance on the stage and that of the actors of a photoplay. The expression of the inner states, the whole system of gestures, is decidedly different, and here we might say that the photoplay stands nearer to life than the pantomime. Of course, the photoplayer must somewhat exaggerate the natural expression. The whole rhythm and intensity of his gestures must be more marked than it would be with actors who accompany their movements by spoken words and who express the meaning of their thoughts and feelings by the content of what they say. Nevertheless, the photoplayer uses the regular channels of mental discharge. He acts simply as a very emotional person might act. But the actor who plays in a pantomime cannot be satisfied with that. He is expected to add something which is entirely unnatural, namely a kind of artificial demonstration of his emotions. He must not only behave like an angry man, but he must behave like a man who is consciously interested in his anger and wants to demonstrate it to others. He exhibits his emotions for the spectators. He really acts theatrically for the benefit of the bystanders. If he did not try to do so, his means of conveying a rich story and a real conflict of human passions would be too meager. The photoplayer, with the rapid changes of scenes, has other possibilities of conveying his intentions. He must not yield to the temptation to play a pantomime on the screen, or he will seriously injure the artistic quality of the reel.

The really decisive distance from bodily reality, however, is created by the substitution of the actor's picture for the actor himself. Lights and shades replace the manifoldness of color effects and mere perspective must furnish the suggestion of depth. We traced it when we discussed the psychology of kinematoscopic perception. But we must not put the emphasis on the wrong point. The natural tendency might be to lay the chief stress on the fact that those people in the photoplay do not stand before us in flesh and blood. The essential point is rather that we are conscious of the flatness of the picture. If we were to see the actors of the stage in a mirror, it would also be a reflected image which we perceive. We should not really have the actors themselves in our straight line of vision; and yet this image would appear to us equivalent to the actors themselves, because it would contain all the depth of the real stage. The film picture is such a reflected rendering of the actors. The process which leads from the living men to the screen is more complex than a mere reflection in a mirror, but, in spite of the complexity in the transmission, we do, after all, see the real actor in the picture. The photograph is absolutely different from those pictures which a clever draughtsman has sketched. In the photoplay we see the actors themselves, and the decisive factor which makes the impression different from seeing real men is not that we see the living persons through the medium of photographic reproduction, but that this reproduction shows them in a flat form. The bodily space has been eliminated. We said once before that stereoscopic arrangements could reproduce somewhat this plastic form also. Yet this would seriously interfere with the character of the photoplay. We need there this overcoming of the depth, we want to have it as a picture only and yet as a picture which strongly suggests to us the actual depth of the real world. We want to keep the interest in the plastic world and want to be aware of the depth in which the persons move, but our direct object of perception must be without the depth. That idea of space which forces on us most strongly the idea of heaviness, solidity and substantiality must be replaced by the light flitting immateriality.

But the photoplay sacrifices not only the space values of the real theater; it disregards no less its order of time. The theater presents its plot in the time order of reality. It may interrupt the continuous flow of time without neglecting the conditions of the dramatic art. There may be twenty years between the third and the fourth act, inasmuch as the dramatic writer must select those elements spread over space and time which are significant for the development of his story. But he is bound by the fundamental principle of real time, that it can move only forward and not backward. Whatever the theater shows us now must come later in the story than that which it showed us in any previous moment. The strict classical demand for complete unity of time does not fit every drama, but a drama would give up its mission if it told us in the third act something which happened before the second act. Of course, there may be a play within a play, and the players on the stage which is set on the stage may play events of old Roman history before the king of France. But this is an enclosure of the past in the present, which corresponds exactly to the actual order of events. The photoplay, on the other hand, does not and must not respect this temporal structure of the physical universe. At any point the photoplay interrupts the series and brings us back to the past. We studied this unique feature of the film art when we spoke of the psychology of memory and imagination. With the full freedom of our fancy, with the whole mobility of our association of ideas, pictures of the past flit through the scenes of the present. Time is left behind. Man becomes boy; today is interwoven with the day before yesterday. The freedom of the mind has triumphed over the unalterable law of the outer world.

It is interesting to watch how playwrights nowadays try to steal the thunder of the photoplay and experiment with time reversals on the legitimate stage. We are aesthetically on the borderland when a grandfather tells his grandchild the story of his own youth as a warning, and instead of the spoken words the events of his early years come before our eyes. This is, after all, quite similar to a play within a play. A very different experiment is tried in *Under Cover*. The third act, which plays on the second floor of the house, ends with an explosion. The fourth act, which plays downstairs, begins a quarter of an hour before the explosion. Here we have a real denial of a fundamental condition of the theater. Or if we stick to recent products of the American stage, we may think of *On Trial*, a play which perhaps comes nearest to a dramatic usurpation of the rights of the photoplay. We see the court scene and, as one witness after another begins to give his testimony, the courtroom is replaced by the scenes of the actions about which the witness is to report. Another clever play, *Between the Lines*, ends the first act with a postman bringing three letters from the three children of the house. The second, third, and fourth acts lead us to the three different homes from which the letters came, and the action in the three places not only precedes the writing of the letters, but goes on at the same time. The last act, finally, begins with the arrival of the letters which tell the ending of those events in the three homes. Such experiments are very suggestive, but they are not any longer pure dramatic art. It is always possible to mix arts. An Italian painter produces very striking effects by putting pieces of glass and stone and rope into his paintings, but they are no longer pure paintings. The drama in which the later event comes before the earlier is an aesthetic barbarism which is entertaining as a clever trick in a graceful superficial play, but intolerable in ambitious dramatic art. It is not only tolerable but perfectly natural in any photoplay. The pictorial reflection of the world is not bound by the rigid mechanism of time. Our mind is here and there, our mind turns to the present and then to the past: the photoplay can equal it in its freedom from the bondage of the material world.

But the theater is bound not only by space and time. Whatever it shows is controlled by the same laws of causality which govern nature. This involves a complete continuity of the physical events: no cause without following effect, no effect without preceding cause. This whole natural course is left behind in the play on the screen. The deviation from reality begins with that resolution of the continuous movement which we studied in our psychological discussions. We saw that the impression of movement results from an activity of the mind which binds the separate pictures together. What we actually see is a composite; it is like the movement of a fountain in which every jet is resolved into numberless drops. We feel the play of those drops in their sparkling haste as one continuous stream of water and, yet, are conscious of the myriads of drops, each one separate from the others. This fountainlike spray of pictures has completely overcome the causal world.

In an entirely different form, this triumph over causality appears in the interruption of the events by pictures which belong to another series. We find this whenever the scene suddenly changes. The processes are not carried to their natural consequences. A movement is started, but, before the cause brings its results, another scene has taken its place. What this new scene brings may be an effect for which we saw no causes. But not only the processes are interrupted. The intertwining of the scenes which we have traced in detail is itself such a contrast to causality. It is as if different objects could fill the same space at the same time. It is as if the resistance of the material world had disappeared, and the substances could penetrate one another. In the interlacing of our ideas, we experience this superiority to all physical laws. The theater would not have even the technical means to give us such impressions, but if it had, it would have no right to make use of them, as it would destroy the basis on which the drama is built. We have only another case of the same type in those series of pictures which aim to force a suggestion on our mind. We have spoken of them. A certain effect is prepared by a chain of causes, and yet when the causal result is to appear, the film is cut off. We have the causes without the effect. The villain thrusts with his dagger—but a miracle has snatched away his victim.

While the moving pictures are lifted above the world of space and time and causality and are freed from its bounds, they are certainly not without law. We said before that the freedom with which the pictures replace one another is to a large degree comparable to the sparkling and streaming of the musical tones. The yielding to the play of the mental energies, to the attention and emotion, which is felt in the film pictures, is still more complete in the musical melodies and harmonies in which the tones themselves are merely the expressions of the ideas and feelings and will impulses of the mind. Their harmonies and disharmonies, their fusing and blending, is not controlled by any outer necessity, but by the inner agreement and disagreement of our free impulses. And yet, in this world of musical freedom, everything is completely controlled by aesthetic necessities. No sphere of practical life stands under such rigid rules as the realm of the composer. However bold the musical genius may be, he cannot emancipate himself from the iron rule that his work must show complete unity in itself. All the separate prescriptions which the musical student has to learn are ultimately only the consequences of this central demand which music, the freest of the arts, shares with all the others. In the case of the film, too, the freedom from the physical forms of space, time, and causality does not mean any liberation from this aesthetic bondage either. On the contrary, just as music is surrounded by more technical rules than literature, the photoplay must be held together by the aesthetic demands still more firmly than is the drama. The arts which are subordinated to the conditions of space, time, and causality find a certain firmness of structure in these material forms which contain an element of outer connectedness. But where these forms are given up and where the freedom of mental play replaces their outer necessity, everything would fall asunder if the aesthetic unity were disregarded.

This unity is, first of all, the unity of action. The demand for it is the same which we know from the drama. The temptation to neglect it is nowhere greater than in the photoplay where outside matter can so easily be introduced or independent interests developed. It is certainly true for the photoplay, as for every work of art, that nothing has the right to existence in its midst which is not internally needed for the unfolding of the unified action. Wherever two plots are given to us, we receive less by far than if we had only one plot. We leave the sphere of valuable art entirely when a unified action is ruined by mixing it with declamation and propaganda which is not organically interwoven with the action itself. It may be still fresh in memory what an aesthetically intolerable helter-skelter performance was offered to the public in *The Battlecry of Peace*. Nothing can be more injurious to the aesthetic cultivation of the people than such performances, which hold the attention of the spectators by ambitious detail and yet destroy their aesthetic sensibility by a complete disregard of the fundamental principle of art, the demand for unity. But we recognized also that this unity involves complete isolation. We annihilate beauty when we link the artistic creation with practical interests and transform the spectator into a selfishly interested bystander. The scenic background of the play is not presented in order that we decide whether we want to spend our next vacation there. The interior decoration of the rooms is not exhibited as a display for a department store. The men and women who carry out the action of the plot must not be people whom we may meet tomorrow on the street. All the threads of the play must be knotted together in the play itself, and none should be connected with our outside interests. A good photoplay must be isolated and complete in itself like a beautiful melody. It is not an advertisement for the newest fashions.

This unity of action involves unity of characters. It has too often been maintained by those who theorize on the photoplay that the development of character is the special task of the drama, while the photoplay, which lacks words, must be satisfied with types. Probably this is only a reflection of the crude state which most photoplays of today have not outgrown. Internally, there is no reason why the means of the photoplay should not allow a rather subtle depicting of complex character. But the chief demand is that the characters remain consistent, that the action be developed according to inner necessity and that the characters themselves be in harmony with the central idea of the plot. However, as soon as we insist on unity, we have no right to think only of the action which gives the content of the play. We cannot make light of the form. As in music, the melody and rhythms belong together; as in painting, not every color combination suits every subject; and as in poetry, not every stanza would agree with every idea, so the photoplay must bring action and pictorial expression into perfect harmony. But this demand repeats itself in every single picture. We take it for granted that the painter balances perfectly the forms in his painting, groups them so that an internal symmetry can be felt and that the lines and curves and colors blend into a unity. Every single picture of the sixteen thousand which are shown to us in one reel ought to be treated with this respect of the pictorial artist for the unity of the forms.

The photoplay shows us a significant conflict of human actions in moving pictures which, freed from the physical forms of space, time, and causality, are adjusted to the free play of our mental experiences and which reach complete isolation from the practical world through the perfect unity of plot and pictorial appearance.

Chapter 10: **The Demands of the Photoplay**

We have found the general formula for the new art of the photoplay. We may turn our attention to some consequences which are involved in this general principle and to some aesthetic demands which result from it. Naturally the greatest of all of them is the one for which no specific prescription can be given, namely the imaginative talent of the scenario writer and the producer. The new art is, in that respect, not different from all the old arts. A Beethoven writes immortal symphonies; a thousand conductors are writing symphonies after the same pattern and after the same technical rules, and yet not one survives the next day. What the great painter or sculptor, composer or poet, novelist or dramatist, gives from the depth of his artistic personality is interesting and significant; and the unity of form and content is natural and perfect. What untalented amateurs produce is trivial and flat; the relation of form and content is forced; the unity of the whole is incomplete. Between these two extremes, any possible degree of approach to the ideal is shown in the history of human arts. It cannot be otherwise with the art of the film. Even the clearest recognition of the specific demands of the photoplay cannot be sufficient to replace original talent or genius. The most slavish obedience to aesthetic demands cannot make a tiresome plot interesting and a trivial action significant. If there is anything which introduces a characteristic element into the creation of the photoplay as against all other arts, it may be found in the undeniable fact that the photoplay always demands the cooperation of two inventive personalities, the scenario writer and the producer. Some collaboration exists in other arts too. The opera demands the poet and the composer; and yet, the text of the opera is a work of literature independent and complete in itself, and the music of the opera has its own life. Again, every musical work demands the performer. The orchestra must play the symphonies, the pianist or the singer must make the melodies living, the actors must play the drama. But the music is a perfect work of art even before it is sung or played on an instrument, just as a drama is complete as a work of literature even if it never reaches the stage. Moreover, it is evident that the realization by actors is needed for the photoplay too. But we may disregard that. What we have in mind is that the work which the scenario writer creates is, in itself, still entirely imperfect and becomes a complete work of art only through the action of the producer. He plays a role entirely different from that of the mere stage manager in the drama. The stage manager carries out what the writer of the drama prescribes, however much his own skill and visual imagination and insight into the demands of the characters may add to the embodiment of the dramatic action. But the producer of the photoplay really must show himself a creative artist, inasmuch as he is the one who actually transforms the plays into pictures. The emphasis in the drama lies on the spoken word, to which the stage manager does not add anything. It is all contained in the lines. In the photoplay, the whole emphasis lies on the picture, and its composition is left entirely to the producing artist.

But the scenario writer must not only have talent for dramatic invention and construction; he must be wide awake to the uniqueness of his task; that is, he must feel at every moment that he is writing for the screen and not for the stage or for a book. And this brings us back to our central argument. He must understand that the photoplay is not a photographed drama, but that it is controlled by psychological conditions of its own. As soon as it is grasped that the film play is not simply a mechanical reproduction of another art but is an art of a special kind, it follows that talents of a special kind must be devoted to it and that nobody ought to feel it beneath his artistic dignity to write scenarios in the service of this new art. No doubt, the moving picture performances today still stand on a low artistic level. Nine tenths of the plays are cheap melodramas or vulgar farces. The question is not how much larger a percentage of really valuable dramas can be found in our theaters. Many of their plays are just as much an appeal to the lowest instincts. But, at least, the theater is not forced to be satisfied with such degrading comedies and pseudotragedies. The world literature of the stage contains an abundance of works of eternal value. It is a purely social and not an aesthetic question, why the theaters around the "White Way" yield to the vulgar taste instead of using the truly beautiful drama for the raising of the public mind. The moving picture theaters face an entirely different situation. Their managers may have the best intentions to give better plays; and yet they are unable to do so because the scenario literature has, so far, nothing which can be compared with the master works of the drama, and nothing of this higher type can be expected or hoped for until the creation of photoplays is recognized as worthy of the highest ideal endeavor.

Nobody denies that the photoplay shares the characteristic features of the drama. Both depend upon the conflict of interests and of acts. These conflicts, tragic or comic, demand a similar development and solution on the stage and on the screen. A mere showing of human activity without conflict might give very pleasant moving pictures of idyllic or romantic character or perhaps of practical interest. The result would be a kind of lyric or epic poem on the screen, or a travelogue, or what not, but it would never shape itself into a photoplay as long as that conflict of human interests which the drama demands was lacking. Yet, as this conflict of will is expressed in the one case by living speaking men, in the other by moving pictures, the difference in the artistic conception must surely be as great as the similarity. Hence one of the supreme demands must be for an original literature of real power and significance in which every thought is generated by the idea of the screen. As long as the photoplays are fed by the literature of the stage, the new art can never come to its own and can never reach its real goal. It is surely no fault of Shakespeare that *Hamlet* and *King Lear* are very poor photoplays. If ever a Shakespeare arises for the screen, his work would be equally unsatisfactory if it were dragged to the stage. *Peer Gynt* is no longer Ibsen's if the actors are dumb.

The novel, in certain respects, fares still worse, but in other respects some degrees better. It is true that, in the superficial literature written for the hour, the demarcation line between dramatic and narrative works is often ignored. The best sellers of the novel counter are often warmed over into successful theater plays, and no society play with a long run on Broadway escapes its transformation into a serial novel for the newspapers. But where literature is at its height, the deep difference can be felt distinctly. The epic art, including the novel, traces the experiences and the development of a character, while the drama is dependent upon the conflict of character. Mere adventures of a personality are never sufficient for a good drama and are not less unsatisfactory for the plot of a photoplay. In the novel, the opposing characters are only a part of the social background which is needed to show the life story of the hero or heroine. They have not the independent significance which is essential for the dramatic conflict. The novel on the screen, if it is a true novel and not the novelistic rendering of what is really a dramatic plot, must be lifeless and uninspiring. But, on the other hand, the photoplay much more than the drama emphasizes the background of human action, and it shares this trait with the novel. Both the social and the natural backgrounds are the real setting for the development of the chief character in the story. These features can easily be transferred to the photoplay, and for this reason, some picturized novels have had the advantage over the photoplay cut from the drama. The only true conclusion must remain, however, that neither drama nor novel is sufficient for the film scenarios. The photopoet must turn to life itself and must remodel life in the artistic forms which are characteristic of his particular art. If he has truly grasped the fundamental meaning of the screen world, his imagination will guide him more safely than his reminiscences of dramas which he has seen on the stage and of novels which he has read.

If we turn to a few special demands which are contained in such a general postulate for a new artistic method, we naturally think at once of the role of words. The drama and novel live by words. How much of this noblest vehicle of thought can the photoplay conserve in its domain? We all know what a large part of the photoplay today is told us by the medium of words and phrases. How little would we know what those people are talking about if we saw them only acting and had not beforehand the information which the "leader" supplies. The technique differs with different companies. Some experiment with projecting the spoken words into the picture itself, bringing the phrase in glaring white letters near the head of the person who is speaking, in a way similar to the methods of the newspaper cartoonists. But mostly the series of the pictures is interrupted and the decisive word taken directly from the lips of the hero, or an explanatory statement which gives meaning to the whole is thrown on the screen. Sometimes, this may be a concession to the mentally less trained members of the audience, but usually, these printed comments are indispensable for understanding the plot, and even the most intelligent spectator would feel helpless without these frequent guideposts. But this habit of the picture houses today is certainly not an aesthetic argument. They are obliged to yield to the scheme simply because the scenario writers are still untrained and clumsy in using the technique of the new art.

Some religious painters of medieval times put in the picture itself phrases which the persons were supposed to speak, as if the words were leaving their mouths. But we could not imagine Raphael and Michelangelo making use of a method of communication, which is so entirely foreign to the real spirit of painting. Every art grows slowly to the point where the artist relies on its characteristic and genuine forms of expression. Elements which do not belong to it are at first mingled in it and must be slowly eliminated. The photoplay of the day after tomorrow will surely be freed from all elements which are not really pictures. The beginning of the photoplay as a mere imitation of the theater is nowhere so evident as in this inorganic combination with bits of dialogue or explanatory phrases. The art of words and the art of pictures are there forcibly yoked together. Whoever writes his scenarios so that the pictures cannot be understood without these linguistic crutches is an aesthetic failure in the new art. The next step

143

toward the emancipation of the photoplay decidedly must be the creation of plays which speak the language of pictures only.

Two apparent exceptions seem justified. It is not contrary to the internal demands of the film art if a complete scene has a title. A leader like "The Next Morning" or "After Three Years" or "In South Africa" or "The First Step" or "The Awakening" or "Among Friends" has the same character as the title of a painting in a picture gallery. If we read in our catalogue of paintings that a picture is called "Landscape" or "Portrait" we feel the words to be superfluous. If we read that its title is "London Bridge in Mist" or "Portrait of the Pope" we receive a valuable suggestion which is surely not without influence on our appreciation of the picture, and yet it is not an organic part of the painting itself. In this sense, a leader as title for a scene or still better for a whole reel may be applied without any aesthetic objection. The other case which is not only possible but perfectly justified is the introduction of letters, telegrams, posters, newspaper clippings, and similar printed or written communications in a pictorial close-up the enlargement of which makes every word readable. This scheme is more and more introduced into the plays today and the movement is in a proper direction. The words of the telegram or of the signboard and even of the cutting from the newspaper are parts of the reality which the pictures are to show us and their meaning does not stand outside but within the pictorial story. The true artist will make sparing use of this method in order that the spectator may not change his attitude. He must remain in an inner adjustment to pictorial forms and must not switch over into an adaptation to sentences. But if its use is not exaggerated, the method is legitimate, in striking contrast to the inartistic use of the same words as leaders between the pictures.

The condemnation of guiding words, in the interest of the purity of the picture play as such, also leads to earnest objection to phonographic accompaniments. Those who, like Edison, had a technical, scientific, and social interest but not a genuine aesthetic point of view in the development of the moving pictures, naturally asked themselves whether this optical imitation of the drama might not be improved by an acoustical imitation too. Then the idea would be to connect the kinematoscope with the phonograph and to synchronize them so completely that with every visible movement of the lips the audible sound of the words would leave the diaphragm of the apparatus. All who devoted themselves to this problem had considerable difficulties, and, when their ventures proved practical failures with the theater audiences, they were inclined to blame their inability to solve the technical problem perfectly. They were not aware that the real difficulty was an aesthetic and internal one. Even if the voices were heard with ideal perfection and exactly in time with the movements on the screen, the effect on an aesthetically conscientious audience would have been disappointing. A photoplay cannot gain but only lose if its visual purity is destroyed. If we see and hear at the same time, we do indeed come nearer to the real theater, but this is desirable only if it is our goal to imitate the stage. Yet if that were the goal, even the best imitation would remain far inferior to an actual theater performance. As soon as we have clearly understood that the photoplay is an art in itself, the conservation of the spoken word is as disturbing as color would be on the clothing of a marble statue.

It is quite different with accompanying music. Even if the music in the overwhelming majority of cases were not so pitifully bad as it is in most of the picture theaters of today, no one would consider it an organic part of the photoplay itself, like the singing in the opera. Yet the need of such a more or less melodious, and even more or less harmonious, accompaniment has always been felt, and even the poorest substitute for decent music has been tolerated, as seeing long reels in a darkened house without any tonal accompaniment fatigues and ultimately irritates an average audience. The music relieves the tension and keeps the attention awake. It must be entirely subordinated, and it is a fact that most people are hardly aware of the special pieces which are played, while they would feel uncomfortable without them. But it is not at all necessary for the music to be limited to such harmonious smoothing of the mind by rhythmical tones. The music can and ought to be adjusted to the play on the screen. The more ambitious picture corporations have clearly recognized this demand and show their new plays with exact suggestions for the choice of musical pieces to be played as accompaniment. The music does not tell a part of the plot and does not replace the picture as words would do, but simply reenforces the emotional setting. It is quite probable, when the photoplay art has found its aesthetic recognition, that composers will begin to write the musical score for a beautiful photoplay with the same enthusiasm with which they write in other musical forms.

Just between the intolerable accompaniment by printed or spoken words on the one side and the perfectly welcome rendering of emotionally fitting music on the other, we find the noises with which the photoplay managers like to accompany their performances. When the horses gallop, we must hear the hoofbeats, if rain or hail is falling, if the lightning flashes, we hear the splashing or the thunderstorm. We hear the firing of a gun, the whistling of a locomotive, ships' bells, or the ambulance gong, or the barking dog, or the noise when Charlie Chaplin falls downstairs. They even have a complicated machine, the "allefex," which can produce over fifty distinctive noises, fit for any photoplay emergency. It will probably take longer to rid the photoplay of these appeals to the imagination than the explanations of the leaders, but ultimately, they will have to disappear too. They have no right to existence in a work of art which is composed of pictures. In so far as they are simply heightening the emotional tension, they may enter into the music itself, but in so far as they tell a part of the story, they ought to be ruled out as intrusions from another sphere. We might just as well improve the painting of a rose garden by bathing it in rose perfume in order that the spectators might get the odor of the roses together with the sight of them. The limitations of an art are in reality its strength and to overstep its boundaries means to weaken it.

It may be more open to discussion whether this same negative attitude ought to be taken toward color in the photoplay. It is well-known that wonderful technical progress has been secured by those who wanted to catch the color hues and tints of nature in their moving pictures. To be sure, many of the prettiest effects in color are even today produced by artificial stencil methods. Photographs are simply printed in three colors like any ordinary color print. The task of cutting those many stencils for the thousands of pictures on a reel is tremendous, and yet these difficulties have been overcome. Any desired color effect can be obtained by this method and the beauty of the best specimens is unsurpassed. But the difficulty is so great that it can hardly become a popular method. The direct photographing of the colors themselves will be much simpler as soon as the method is completely perfected. It can hardly be said that this ideal has been reached today. The successive photographing through three red, green, and violet screens and the later projection of the pictures through screens of these colors seemed scientifically the best approach. Yet it needed a multiplication of pictures per second which offered extreme difficulty, besides an extraordinary increase of expense. The practical advance seems more secure along the line of the so-called "kinemacolor." Its effects are secured by the use of two screens only, not quite satisfactory, as true blue impressions have to suffer and the reddish and greenish ones are emphasized. Moreover the eye is sometimes disturbed by big flashes of red or green light. Yet the beginnings are so excellent that the perfect solution of the technical problem may be expected in the near future. Would it be at the same time a solution of the aesthetic problem?

It has been claimed by friends of color photography that, at the present stage of development, natural color photography is unsatisfactory for a rendering of outer events, because any scientific or historical happening which is reproduced demands exactly the same colors which reality shows. But on the other hand, the process seems perfectly sufficient for the photoplay, because there no objective colors are expected, and it makes no difference whether the gowns of the women or the rugs on the floor show the red and green too vividly and the blue too faintly. From an aesthetic point of view we ought to come to exactly the opposite verdict. For the historical events even the present technical methods are, on the whole, satisfactory. The famous British coronation pictures were superb, and they gained immensely by the rich color effects. They gave much more than a mere photograph in black and white, and the splendor and glory of those radiant colors suffered little from the suppression of the bluish tones. They were not shown in order to match the colors in a ribbon store. For the news pictures of the day the "kinemacolor" and similar schemes are excellent. But when we come to photoplays, the question is no longer one of technique; first of all, we stand before the problem, how far does the coloring subordinate itself to the aim of the photoplay? No doubt the effect of the individual picture would be heightened by the beauty of the colors. But would it heighten the beauty of the photoplay? Would not this color be again an addition which oversteps the essential limits of this particular art? We do not want to paint the cheeks of the Venus of Milo, neither do we want to see the coloring of Mary Pickford or Anita Stewart. We became aware that the unique task of the photoplay art can be fulfilled only by a far-reaching disregard of reality. The real human persons and the real landscapes must be left behind and, as we saw, must be transformed into pictorial suggestions only. We must be strongly conscious of their pictorial unreality in order that that wonderful play of our inner experiences may be realized on the screen. This consciousness of un-reality must seriously suffer from the addition of color. We are once more brought too near to the world which really surrounds us with the richness of its colors, and the more we approach it, the less we gain that inner freedom, that victory of the mind over nature, which remains the ideal of the photoplay. The colors are almost as detri-mental as the voices.

On the other hand the producer must be careful to keep sufficient-ly in contact with reality, as otherwise the emotional interests upon which the whole play depends would be destroyed. We must not take the people to be real, but we must link with them all the feelings and associations which we world connect with real men. This is possible only if in their flat, colorless, pictorial setting they share the real fea-tures of men. For this reason it is important to suggest to the spectator the impression of natural size. The demand of the imagination for the normal size of the persons and things in the picture is so strong that it easily and constantly overcomes great enlargements or reductions. We see at first a man in his normal size and then, by a close-up, an excessive enlargement of his head. Yet we do not feel it as if the person himself were enlarged. By a characteristic psychical substitution, we feel rather that we have come nearer to him and that the size of the visual image was increased by the decreasing of the distance. If the whole picture is so much enlarged that the persons are continually given much above normal size, by a psychical inhibition, we deceive ourselves about the distance and believe that we are much nearer to the screen than we actually are. Thus we instinctively remain under the impression of normal appearances. But this spell can easily be broken, and the aesthetic effect is then greatly diminished. In the large picture houses in which the projecting camera is often very far from the screen, the dimensions of the persons in the pictures may be three or four times larger than human beings. The illusion is nevertheless perfect, because the spectator misjudges the distances as long as he does not see anything in the neighborhood of the screen. But if the eye falls upon a woman playing the piano directly below the picture, the illusion is destroyed. He sees on the screen enormous giants whose hands are as large as half the piano player, and the normal reactions which are the spring for the enjoyment of the play are suppressed.

The further we go into details, the more we might add such special psychological demands which result from the fundamental principles of the new art. But it would be misleading if we were also to raise demands concerning a point which has often played the chief role in the discussion, namely, the selection of suitable topics. Writers who have the unlimited possibilities of trick pictures and film illusions in mind have proclaimed that the fairy tale with its magic wonders ought to be its chief domain, as no theater stage could enter into rivalry. How many have enjoyed *Neptune's Daughter*—the mermaids in the surf and the sudden change of the witch into the octopus on the shore and the joyful play of the watersprites! How many have been bewitched by Princess Nicotina when she trips from the little cigar box along the table! No theater could dare to imitate such raptures of imagination. Other writers have insisted on the superb chances for gorgeous processions and the surging splendor of multitudes. We see thousands in Sherman's march to the sea. How hopeless would be any attempt to imitate on the stage! When the toreador fights the bull and the crowds in the Spanish arena enter into enthusiastic frenzy, who would compare it with those painted people in the arena when the opera *Carmen* is sung? Again others emphasize the opportunity for historical plays or, especially, for plays with unusual scenic setting where the beauties of the tropics or of the mountains, of the ocean or of the jungle, are brought into living contact with the spectator. Biblical dramas with pictures of real Palestine, classical plots with real Greece or Rome as a background, have stirred millions all over the globe. Yet the majority of authors claim that the true field for the photoplay is the practical life which surrounds us, as no artistic means of literature or drama can render the details of life with such convincing sincerity and with such realistic power. These are the slums, not seen through the spectacles of a littérateur or the fancy of an outsider, but in their whole abhorrent nakedness. These are the dark corners of the metropolis where crime is hidden and where vice is growing rankly.

They all are right, and at the same time they all are wrong when they praise one at the expense of another. Realistic and idealistic, practical and romantic, historical and modern topics are fit material for the art of the photoplay. Its world is as unlimited as that of literature, and the same is true of the style of treatment. The humorous, if it is true humor, the tragic, if it is true tragedy, the gay and the solemn, the merry and the pathetic, the half-reel and the five-reel play, all can fulfill the demands of the new art.

Chapter 11: **The Function of the Photoplay**

Enthusiasts claim that in the United States ten million people daily are attending picture houses. Sceptics believe that "only" two or three millions form the daily attendance. But in any case, "the movies" have become the most popular entertainment of the country, nay, of the world, and their influence is one of the strongest social energies of our time. Signs indicate that this popularity and this influence are increasing from day to day. What are the causes, and what are the effects of this movement which was undreamed of only a short time ago?

The economists are certainly right when they see the chief reason for this crowding of picture houses in the low price of admission. For five or ten cents, long hours of thrilling entertainment in the best seats of the house: this is the magnet which must be more powerful than any theater or concert. Yet the rush to the moving pictures is steadily increasing, while the prices climb up. The dime became a quarter, and in the last two seasons ambitious plays were given before audiences who paid the full theater rates. The character of audiences, too, suggests that inexpensiveness alone cannot be decisive. Six years ago a keen sociological observer characterized the patrons of the picture palaces as "the lower middle class and the massive public, youths and shopgirls between adolescence and maturity, small dealers, pedlars, laborers, charwomen, besides the small quota of children." This would be hardly a correct description today. This "lower middle class" has long been joined by the upper middle class. To be sure, our observer of that long forgotten past added meekly: "Then there emerges a superior person or two like yourself attracted by mere curiosity and kept in his seat by interest until the very end of the performance; this type sneers aloud to proclaim its superiority and preserve its self-respect, but it never leaves the theater until it must." Today, you and I are seen there quite often, and we find that our friends have been there, that they have given up the sneering pose and talk about the new photoplay as a matter of course.

Above all, even those who are drawn by the cheapness of the performance would hardly push their dimes under the little window so often if they did not really enjoy the plays and were not stirred by a pleasure which holds them for hours. After all, it must be the content of the performances which is decisive of the incomparable triumph. We have no right to conclude from this that only the merits and excellences are the true causes of their success. A caustic critic would probably suggest that just the opposite traits are responsible. He would say that the average American is a mixture of business, ragtime, and sentimentality. He satisfies his business instinct by getting so much for his nickel, he enjoys his ragtime in the slapstick humor, and gratifies his sentimentality with the preposterous melodramas which fill the program. This is quite true, and yet it is not true at all. Success has crowned every effort to improve the photostage; the better the plays are the more the audience approves them. The most ambitious companies are the most flourishing ones. There must be inner values which make the photoplay so extremely attractive and even fascinating.

To a certain degree the mere technical cleverness of the pictures even today holds the interest spellbound, as in those early days when nothing but this technical skill could claim the attention. We are still startled by every original effect, even if the mere showing of movement has today lost its impressiveness. Moreover we are captivated by the undeniable beauty of many settings. The melodrama may be cheap; yet it does not disturb the cultured mind as grossly as a similar tragic vulgarity would on the real stage, because it may have the snowfields of Alaska or the palm trees of Florida as radiant background. An intellectual interest, too, finds its satisfaction. We get an insight into spheres which were strange to us. Where outlying regions of human interest are shown on the theater stage, we must usually be satisfied with some standardized suggestion. Here in the moving pictures, the play may really bring us to mills and factories, to farms and mines, to courtrooms and hospitals, to castles and palaces in any land on earth.

Yet a stronger power of the photoplay probably lies in its own dramatic qualities. The rhythm of the play is marked by unnatural rapidity. As the words are absent which, in the drama as in life, fill the gaps between the actions, the gestures and deeds themselves can follow one another much more quickly. Happenings which would fill an hour on the stage can hardly fill more than twenty minutes on the screen. This heightens the feeling of vitality in the spectator. He feels as if he were passing through life with a sharper accent which stirs his personal energies. The usual make-up of the photoplay must strengthen this effect inasmuch as the wordlessness of the picture drama favors a certain simplification of the social conflicts. The subtler shades of the motives naturally demand speech. The later plays of Ibsen could hardly be transformed into photoplays. Where words are missing, the characters tend to become stereotyped and the motives to be deprived of their complexity. The plot of the photoplay is usually based on the fundamental emotions which are common to all and which are understood by everybody. Love and hate, gratitude and envy, hope and fear, pity and jealousy, repentance and sinfulness, and all the similar crude emotions have been sufficient for the construction of most scenarios. The more mature development of the photoplay will certainly overcome this primitive character, as, while such an effort to reduce human life to simple instincts is very convenient for the photoplay, it is not at all necessary. In any case, where this tendency prevails it must help greatly to excite and to intensify the personal feeling of life and to stir the depths of the human mind.

But the richest source of the unique satisfaction in the photoplay is probably that aesthetic feeling which is significant for the new art and which we have understood from its psychological conditions. *The massive outer world has lost its weight, it has been freed from space, time, and causality, and it has been clothed in the forms of our own consciousness. The mind has triumphed over matter, and the pictures roll on with the ease of musical tones. It is a superb enjoyment which no other art can furnish us.* No wonder that temples for the new goddess are built in every little hamlet.

The intensity with which the plays take hold of the audience cannot remain without strong social effects. It has even been reported that sensory hallucinations and illusions have crept in; neurasthenic persons are especially inclined to experience touch or temperature or smell or sound impressions from what they see on the screen. The associations become as vivid as realities, because the mind is so completely given up to the moving pictures. The applause into which the audiences, especially of rural communities, break out at a happy turn of the melodramatic pictures is another symptom of the strange fascination. But it is evident that such a penetrating influence must be fraught with dangers. The more vividly the impressions force themselves on the mind, the more easily must they become starting points for imitation and other motor responses. The sight of crime and of vice may force itself on the consciousness with disastrous results. The normal resistance breaks down and the moral balance, which would have been kept under the habitual stimuli of the narrow routine life, may be lost under the pressure of the realistic suggestions. At the same time, the subtle sensitiveness of the young mind may suffer from the rude contrasts between the farces and the passionate romances which follow with benumbing speed in the darkened house. The possibilities of psychical infection and destruction cannot be overlooked. Those may have been exceptional cases only when grave crimes have been traced directly back to the impulses from unwholesome photoplays, but no psychologist can determine exactly how much the general spirit of righteousness, of honesty, of sexual cleanliness and modesty, may be weakened by the unbridled influence of plays of low moral standard. All countries seem to have been awakened to this social danger. The time when unsavory French comedies poisoned youth lies behind us. A strong reaction has set in, and the leading companies among the photoplay producers fight everywhere in the first rank for suppression of the unclean. Some companies even welcome censorship, provided that it is high-minded and liberal and does not confuse artistic freedom with moral licentiousness. Most, to be sure, seem doubtful whether the new movement toward Federal censorship is in harmony with American ideas on the freedom of public expression.

But while the sources of danger cannot be overlooked, the social reformer ought to focus his interest still more on the tremendous influences for good which may be exerted by the moving pictures. The fact that millions are daily under the spell of the performances on the screen is established. The high degree of their suggestibility during those hours in the dark house may be taken for granted. Hence any wholesome influence emanating from the photoplay must have an incomparable power for the remolding and upbuilding of the national soul. From this point of view, the boundary lines between the photoplay and the merely instructive moving pictures with the news of the day or the magazine articles on the screen become effaced. The intellectual, the moral, the social, and the aesthetic culture of the community may be served by all of them. Leading educators have joined in endorsing the foundation of a Universal Culture Lyceum. The plan is to make, and circulate moving pictures for the education of the youth of the land, picture studies in science, history, religion, literature, geography, biography, art, architecture, social science, economics, and industry. From this Lyceum "schools, churches, and colleges will be furnished with motion pictures giving the latest results and activities in every sphere capable of being pictured."

But, however much may be achieved by such conscious efforts toward education, the far larger contribution must be made by the regular picture houses which the public seeks without being conscious of the educational significance. The teaching of the moving pictures must not be forced on a more or less indifferent audience, but ought to be absorbed by those who seek entertainment and enjoyment from the films and are ready to make their little economic sacrifice.

The purely intellectual part of this uplift is the easiest. Not only the news pictures and the scientific demonstrations, but also the photoplay can lead young and old to ever new regions of knowledge. The curiosity and the imagination of the spectators will follow gladly. Yet, even in the intellectual sphere, the dangers must not be overlooked. They are not positive. It is not as in the moral sphere where the healthy moral impulse is checked by the sight of crimes which stir up antisocial desires. The danger is not that the pictures open insight into facts which ought not be to known. It is not the dangerous knowledge which must be avoided, but it is the trivializing influence of a steady contact with things which are not worth knowing. The larger part of the film literature of today is certainly harmful in this sense. The intellectual background of most photoplays is insipid. By telling the plot without the subtle motivation which the spoken word of the drama may bring, not only do the characters lose color but all the scenes and situations are simplified to a degree which adjusts them to a thoughtless public and soon becomes intolerable to an intellectually trained spectator.

They force on the cultivated mind that feeling which musical persons experience in the musical comedies of the day. We hear the melodies constantly with the feeling of having heard them ever so often before. This lack of originality and inspiration is not necessary; it does not lie in the art form. Offenbach and Strauss and others have written musical comedies which are classical. Neither does it lie in the form of the photoplay that the story must be told in that insipid, flat, uninspired fashion. Nor is it necessary in order to reach the millions. To appeal to the intelligence does not mean to presuppose college education. Moreover, the differentiation has already begun. Just as the plays of Shaw or Ibsen address a different audience from that reached by *The Old Homestead* or *Ben Hur*, we have already photoplays adapted to different types, and there is not the slightest reason to connect with the art of the screen an intellectual flabbiness. It would be no gain for intellectual culture if all the reasoning were confined to the so-called instructive pictures and the photoplays were served without any intellectual salt. On the contrary, the appeal of those strictly educational lessons may be less deep than the producers hope, because the untrained minds, especially of youth and of the uneducated audiences, have considerable difficulty in following the rapid flight of events when they occur in unfamiliar surroundings. The child grasps very little in seeing the happenings in a factory. The psychological and economic lesson may be rather wasted, because the power of observation is not sufficiently developed and the assimilation proceeds too slowly. But it is quite different when a human interest stands behind it and connects the events in the photoplay.

The difficulties in the way of the right moral influence are still greater than in the intellectual field. Certainly it is not enough to have the villain punished in the last few pictures of the reel. If scenes of vice or crime are shown with all their lure and glamour, the moral devastation of such a suggestive show is not undone by the appended social reaction. The misguided boys or girls feel sure that they would be successful enough not to be trapped. The mind, through a mechanism which has been understood better and better by the psychologists in recent years, suppresses the ideas which are contrary to the secret wishes and makes those ideas flourish by which those "subconscious" impulses are fulfilled. It is probably a strong exaggeration when a prominent criminologist recently claimed that "eighty-five per cent of the juvenile crime which has been investigated has been found traceable either directly or indirectly to motion pictures which have shown on the screen how crimes could be committed." But certainly, as far as these demonstrations have worked havoc, their influence would not have been annihilated by a picturesque court scene in which the burglar is unsuccessful in misleading the jury. The true moral influence must come from the positive spirit of the play itself. Even the photodramatic lessons in temperance and piety will not rebuild a frivolous or corrupt or perverse community. The truly upbuilding play is not a dramatized sermon on morality and religion.

There must be a moral wholesomeness in the whole setting, a moral atmosphere which is taken as a matter of course like fresh air and sunlight. An enthusiasm for the noble and uplifting, a belief in duty and discipline of the mind, a faith in ideals and eternal values must permeate the world of the screen. If it does, there is no crime and no heinous deed which the photoplay may not tell with frankness and sincerity. It is not necessary to deny evil and sin in order to strengthen the consciousness of eternal justice.

But the greatest mission which the photoplay may have in our community is that of aesthetic cultivation. No art reaches a larger audience daily, no aesthetic influence finds spectators in a more receptive frame of mind. On the other hand, no training demands a more persistent and planful arousing of the mind than the aesthetic training, and never is progress more difficult than when the teacher adjusts himself to the mere liking of the pupils. The country today would still be without any symphony concerts and operas if it had only received what the audiences believed at the moment that they liked best. The aesthetically commonplace will always triumph over the significant, unless systematic efforts are made to reinforce the work of true beauty. Communities at first always prefer Sousa to Beethoven. The moving picture audience could only by slow steps be brought from the tasteless and vulgar eccentricities of the first period to the best plays of today, and the best plays of today can be nothing but the beginning of the great upward movement which we hope for in the photoplay. Hardly any teaching can mean more for our community than the teaching of beauty where it reaches the masses. The moral impulse and the desire for knowledge are, after all, deeply implanted in the American crowd, but the longing for beauty is rudimentary, and yet, it means harmony, unity, true satisfaction, and happiness in life. The people still have to learn the great difference between true enjoyment and fleeting pleasure, between real beauty and the mere tickling of the senses.

Of course, there are those, and they may be legion today, who would deride every plan to make the moving pictures the vehicle of aesthetic education. How can we teach the spirit of true art by a medium which is in itself the opposite of art? How can we implant the idea of harmony by that which is in itself a parody on art? We hear the contempt for "canned drama" and the machine-made theater. Nobody stops to think whether other arts despise the help of technique. The printed book of lyric poems is also machine-made; the marble bust has also "preserved" for two thousand years the beauty of the living woman who was the model for the Greek sculptor. They tell us that the actor on the stage gives the human beings as they are in reality, but the moving pictures are unreal and, therefore, of incomparably inferior value. They do not consider that the roses of the summer which we enjoy in the stanzas of the poet do not exist in reality in the forms of iambic verse and of rhymes; they live in color and odor, but their color and odor fade away, while the roses in the stanzas live on forever. They fancy that the value of an art depends upon its nearness to the reality of physical nature.

It has been the chief task of our whole discussion to prove the shallowness of such arguments and objections. We recognized that art is a way to overcome nature and to create out of the chaotic material of the world something entirely new, entirely unreal, which embodies perfect unity and harmony. The different arts are different ways of abstracting from reality; and when we began to analyze the psychology of the moving pictures, we soon became aware that the photoplay has a way to perform this task of art with entire originality, independent of the art of the theater, as much as poetry is independent of music or sculpture of painting. It is an art in itself. Only the future can teach us whether it will become a great art, whether a Leonardo, a Shakespeare, a Mozart, will ever be born for it. Nobody can foresee the directions which the new art may take. Mere aesthetic insight into the principles can never foreshadow the development in the unfolding of civilization. Who would have been bold enough four centuries ago to foresee the musical means and effects of the modern orchestra? Just the history of music shows how the inventive genius has always had to blaze the path in which the routine work of the art followed. Tone combinations which appeared intolerable dissonances to one generation were again and again assimilated and welcomed and finally accepted as a matter of course by later times. Nobody can foresee the ways which the new art of the photoplay will open, but everybody ought to recognize, even today, that it is worth while to help this advance, and to make the art of the film a medium for an original creative expression of our time, and to mold by it the aesthetic instincts of the millions. Yes, it is a new art—and this is why it has such fascination for the psychologist who in a world of ready-made arts, each with a history of many centuries, suddenly finds a new form still undeveloped and hardly understood. For the first time the psychologist can observe the starting of an entirely new aesthetic development, a new form of true beauty in the turmoil of a technical age, created by its very technique and yet more than any other art destined to overcome outer nature by the free and joyful play of the mind.

NOTES

1.   Münsterberg's reference here is Peter Mark Roget, "Explanation of an Optical Deception in the Appearance of the Spokes of a Wheel Seen Through Vertical Apertures," *Philosophical Transactions of the Royal Society of London* 115 (1825), pt. 1, 131–140. Both Roget and Joseph Plateau are often given credit for the invention of the Phenakistoscope. For the work of Joseph Antoine Ferdinand Plateau (1801–1883) see his *Dissertation sur quelques propriétés des impressions produites par la lumiere sur l'organe de la vue* (Liege: Dessain, 1829). [Unless otherwise indicated, notes are by the editor.]

2.   He is referring to the article title from Michael Faraday, "On a Particular Class of Optical Deception," *Journal of the Royal Institution* 1 (1831): 205–223, 334–336. This journal only lasted two volumes. Thanks to Frank A. J. L. James of the Royal Institution for this citation.

3.   Münsterberg is probably referring to Simon Ritter von Stampfer's *Die stroboscophishen Scheiben* (Wein: Trentsensky & Vieweg, 1833), on his Stroboscope, invented in 1832.

4. Baron Franz von Uchatius (1811–1881), in 1853 the first person to project images on a screen using a modified version of Plateau's Phenakistoscope.

5. William George Horner (1786–1837). Horner's Daedaleum (literally 'Devil's Wheel') was adapted from Roget's—or Plateau's; the invention is sometimes given to both—Phenakistoscope.

6. Etienne-Jules Marey (1830–1904), like Muybridge, was interested in using photography to record movement. See Virgilio Tosi, "Etienne-Jules Marey and the Origins of Cinema," in *Marey: Pionnier de la Synthèse du Mouvement* (Beaune: Musée Marey, 1995): 76–81; Marta Braun's *Picturing Time: The Work of Etienne-Jules Marey* (Chicago: University of Chicago Press, 1992); and Michael Frizot, *Avant le cinématographe: la chronophotographie, temps, photographie et mouvement autour de E.-J. Marey* (Beaune: Association des Amis de Marey, 1984). See also Etienne-Jules Marey's own work in *Animal Mechanism: A treatise on terrestrial and aerial locomotion* (London: H. S. King, 1874); *La chronophotographie* (Paris: Gauthier-Villas, 1899); *Du mouvement dans les fonctions de la vie* (Paris: Bailliere, 1868); and *Movement*, trans. Eric Pritchard (New York: Arno Press, 1972).

Münsterberg mentions "Marey's tambour," which was a mechanism constructed of rubber tubes connected to a tympanum or membrane of thin rubber which could pneumatically (rather than mechanically) register changes in pressure and or movement. The devices could be adapted to myriad situations. See Braun pp. 20–21.

7. Pierre Jules César Janssen (1824–1907). Janssen's gun-like camera had a rotating photographic plate that shot an exposure of the sun (with Venus in transit across it, in one of his most famous experiments) on a timer every few seconds. His work was compiled in 1904, the year of his death, in his *Atlas des photographies solaires*, which contained more than 6000 pictures of the sun.

8. Ottomar Anschütz (1846–1907), was the inventor of the "Projecting Electrotachyscope."

9. Robert William Paul (1869–1943). British scientist, optician, and electrical engineer who made an English version of Edison's Kinetoscope. He went into film production and was quite successful. He made many technical innovations in projecting technology.

10. I have been unable to confirm with certainty all the experimenters Münsterberg is referring to here. Among those who are identifiable are Siegmund Exner (1846–1926), an Austrian scientist who did experiments on motion sensation. William James is also mentioned, as is Karl Marbe (1869–1953), who wrote a book called *Theorie der kinematographiscen Projektionen* (Leipzig: J. A. Barth, 1910). Max Wertheimer (1880–1943) is known as one of the founders of the Gestalt school of psychology, and A. Korte, who discovered what is known as "Korte's Laws" having to do with the impression of motion. Both Wertheimer and Korte explained the *phi* phenomenon, whereby the illusion of motion is created by two lights successively flashed

at speeds sufficient to fool the eye and mind. Korte's specific analysis of film can be found in his "Kinematoskopische Untersuchungen," *Zeitschrift für Psychologie* 72 (1915): 194–296. Wertheimer's work, in the same journal, had been published 3 years before as "Experimentelle Studien über das Sehen von Bewegung," *Zeitschrift für Psychologie* 61 (1912): 161–265. Münsterberg refers also to L. William Stern, probably the article "Die Wahrnehmung von Bewegungen vermittelst des Auge," *Zeitschrift für Psychologie* 7 (1894): 321–385; and Paul Linke's "Die stroboskopische Täuschungen und das Problem des Sehens von Bewegungen," *Psychologie Studie* 3 (1907). Linke's major work followed a year later in his *Grundfragen der Wahrnehmungslehr* of 1918.

Additional Writings and Texts

Margaret Münsterberg
on *The Photoplay*

Münsterberg's pioneer spirit was not content. A new interest had taken hold of him, one that appealed at the same time to the psychologist and to the lover of art—an interest in the photoplay. In this new study Münsterberg sought distraction for himself from the wearing anxieties caused by the international stress, and at the same time hoped to make the imagination of the public link his name with a more serene interest.

Münsterberg had not been a "movie" patron; indeed, he had looked upon motion pictures, with the exception of travel pictures like *Ramy's Hunt*, as rather in a class with vaudeville, which he never approached. On a journey, however, he saw Annette Kellermann's mermaid pranks in *Neptune's Daughter*, and this not only delighted him, but opened his eyes to the distinctive character and possibilities of the photoplay. During the summer of 1915 he spent many hours in motion-picture houses. In June of that year the Vitagraph Company in New York showed him, with ready hospitality, its studios, its methods, its actors and actresses. A snapshot picture was taken of Münsterberg listening attentively to Anita Stewart. He was an eager pupil and the more he studied this fascinating field, the more he was convinced of the uniqueness of its artistic mission. The photoplay was not, what it first seemed to be, a substitute for the spoken drama, any more than sculpture is a substitute for painting. Since all art is a representation of life, with certain definite limitations, so the photoplay is defined by the absence of depth and color and voice, yet given infinite possibilities of expression through its peculiar attributes. There is the

From Margaret Münsterberg, *Hugo Münsterberg: His Life and Work* (New York & London: D. Appleton & Co., 1922): 281–287.

power of commanding attention toward some isolated detail through the use of the "close-up"; there is the reinforcement of memory through flashing scenes of bygone events into the midst of the story; there is the freedom from the limitations of space, by which simultaneous events may be shown in quickly alternating pictures; emotional effects may be heightened by the rapid and skillful succession of scenes. All in all, the photoplay has its own characteristics, its own possibilities, and there is no reason why these should not be utilized in the service of the highest art.

In the *Cosmopolitan Magazine* for December, 1915, Münsterberg published a popular article called "Why We Go to the Movies" which heralded his book on the subject. Between October and the end of December, 1915, Münsterberg wrote a volume of 232 pages that appeared in April, 1916, under the title *The Photoplay, a Psychological Study*. This book contains an Introduction of two chapters that gives the history of the moving-picture art: one the history of the outer, that is, the technical, development from the first simple devices for producing the illusion of movement, invented in the first half of the 19th century; the other, the history of the inner development, that is, of the contents of the pictures after the perfection of the technique had granted free scope to the imagination. After the Introduction, the book is divided into two parts, "The Psychology of the Photoplay" and "The Aesthetics of the Photoplay." In the first part the psychologist explains the mental processes of the spectator as affected by the ways and means of the moving pictures. Thus he discusses the perception of depth and movement, the acts of attention, the effect of photoplay devices on the memory and the imagination and finally on the emotion. Such an explanation of the part that the human mind itself plays when it enjoys a performance was the contribution of the scientific psychologist. Yet the philosopher in Münsterberg never allowed the scientist to say the last word on any problem of real life. It is the philosopher and the lover of beauty who, in the first chapter of the second part, sets forth "The Purpose of Art." "The work of art shows us the things and events perfectly complete in themselves, freed from all connections which lead beyond their own limits; that is, in perfect isolation." This isolation is to secure that harmony and perfection which only rare moments of real life can give. "That restful happiness which the beautiful landscape or the harmonious life relation can furnish us in blessed instants of our struggling life is secured as a joy forever when the painter or the sculptor, the dramatist or the poet, the composer or the photoplaywright, recomposes nature and life and shows us a unity which does not lead beyond itself, but is in itself perfectly harmonious." Artistic isolation requires some restriction in the means of reproducing life; and these limitations accordingly are the source of strength in any form of art. "A work of art may and must start from something which awakens in us the interests of reality and which contains traits of reality, and to that extent it cannot avoid some imitation. But it becomes art just in so far as it overcomes reality, stops imitating and leaves the imitated reality behind it." These conditions the photoplay, with its obvious limitations, fulfills, and rises thereby far above an imitation of the spoken drama. "The drama and the photoplay are two coordinated arts, each perfectly valuable in itself." A consideration of "The Means of the Various Arts" leads to a study of the peculiar "Means of the Photoplay." This youngest of the arts is neither music nor drama nor painting; but "it shares something with all of them" and it has its own laws. The conclusion at which we arrive is that "the photoplay shows us a significant conflict of human actions in moving pictures which, freed from the physical forms of space, time, and causality, are adjusted to the free play of our mental experiences and which reach complete isolation from the practical world through the perfect unity of plot and pictorial appearance." We realize the need of serious photoplay writing by true "photopoets" who recognize the special demands of the art, so that the dramatization of novels or the bringing on to the screen of plays not intended for it will no longer be necessary; we realize also that long explanatory leaders should be eliminated as much as possible, and good accompanying music should be introduced. Finally, in "The Function of the Photoplay," we are reminded of the great power for good which a form of entertainment that appeals to great masses may exert. This good lies not so much in the instruction that the pictures may impart, or in the morally wholesome air that they may and ought to offer, but more especially in the education for true beauty. "Only the future can teach us whether it will become a great art, whether a Leonardo, a Shakespeare, a Mozart will ever be born for it." Yet "for the first time the psychologist can observe the starting of an entirely new aesthetic development, a new form of true beauty in the turmoil of a technical age, created by its very technique and yet more than any other art destined to overcome outer nature by the free and joyful play of the mind."

Münsterberg's great hope for the future of the moving pictures thus centered round the photoplay as art. Nevertheless he thought the plan of making it a vehicle for public instruction also worthy of encouragement. When the Paramount Company started its Pictographs or the "magazine on the screen" for public instruction in science, history, current events, etc., it asked Münsterberg to be among the first contributors. The psychologist prepared a series of pictures which he called "Testing the Mind" and which were to introduce a new element, namely, the active mental participation of the audience. The methods of testing attention, memory, constructive imagination, capacity for making quick estimates, etc., which he had worked out for purposes of vocational guidance, were now presented in the form of pictures. A puzzle, as, for instance, a jumble of letters, which, if assorted, would spell the name of a city, or a room full of people whose number is to be estimated, is thrown upon the screen and, after an exposure long enough to let the audience answer the question, the correct solution is given. This unique feature was received with enthusiasm. An ardent article in "Motography" expressed the significance of the novelty in this way: "Intellectually, the world has been divided into two classes—the 'highbrows' and the 'lowbrows.' The Pictograph will bring these two brows together." Münsterberg also began to work out graphic ways of presenting history on the screen, but his efforts in this direction were never completed.

His new interest in this cheerful art brought Münsterberg many letters from men who had the future of the moving pictures at heart, letters that he thoroughly enjoyed. A letter to Mr. Edwards is merely an example of the correspondence that afforded him much pleasure.

Cambridge, Massachusetts,
April 5, 1916.

My Dear sir:
In going over some piles of old letters, I stumble upon a letter from you written on February 16th which bears no mark of having been answered. If that is the case, I am very sorry that you remained six weeks without reply. Yet as your problem is not one for a single day or week, a word of interest in your plans may still be in order.

I have given much attention to moving-picture problems in recent times. The book *The Photoplay: A Psychological Study*, which will appear at the end of this week with D. Appleton and Co., New York, is an external symptom of it. But I have also approached your special field, the educational picture, inasmuch as I have furnished the Paramount Pictures Corporation with material for a series of psychological tests on the screen, which appear in their weekly Paramount Pictograph. As far as I can judge, these psychological test demonstrations in moving-picture form have stirred up a very considerable interest for mental life in many cities, and this success encourages me greatly in the belief that the film can become a tremendous educational agency.

For this reason I endorse most heartily your plan to specialize in educational films. The idea of presenting the Montessori system, for instance, seems to me excellent, and every movement toward bringing geography to the attention of the masses in a striking way certainly deserves the warmest sympathy, as the defects of popular education are nowhere so glaring as in geography.

I think the greatest trouble in the moving-picture world today is the lack of discrimination and differentiation. While everybody in a large city knows which theatres appeal to serious taste and which to mere vulgarity, or which magazines are of high value and which are cheap and trivial, nobody knows what he will get in the next moving-picture show. This lack of differentiation is certainly a symptom of the crude state of the moving-picture industry as yet. In a few years such differentiation will be demanded everywhere, and one of the first steps toward it ought to be a clean division of labor among the producing companies. I welcome it as a very promising step that you intend to specialize in the educational field and to set this off as a great work of its own, separated from the mere amusement plays. Your chances are tremendous. I think there is hardly a science which could not be cleverly presented in fascinating moving pictures. I shall be very glad to hear from you again.

Very truly yours,
Hugo Münsterberg

Münsterberg was now invited to speak on the Psychology of the Photoplay. An article on "Moving Pictures and the Child" appeared in the *Mother's Magazine*, to which Münsterberg previously contributed essays on vocational guidance for boys and girls. But talking and writing was not enough; the moving-picture world, now that Münsterberg had become one of its champions, did not let him rest, but made him a judge of one of its prize contests. The *Traveler Herald* offered prizes to the public for the best scenarios, and Münsterberg was to be one of the five judges together with Winthrop Ames, E. Winthrop Sargent, Leon Dadmun, and Miss Salita Solano. On a hot summer night on his veranda in Clifton, he read the thirty scenarios sifted from the great bulk of competing literature, and shook his head in wonder at the poor quality. Within the last weeks of his life he attended the "movie ball" at which the prizes for the competition were given, sitting in a box for the judges of the contest.

Why We Go to the Movies

Hugo Münsterberg

The "movies" themselves are moving all the time. To be sure, they move on different roads. One road is that of education and instruction. How modest were the means with which the kinematoscope of fifteen years ago showed us the happenings of the world and gave us glances at current events and exhibited a little of animal life! It was a long way indeed from there to the marvelous pictures of the European war or to those fascinating moving-picture journeys to the Antarctic and to the beasts of the African desert. We all have seen the wonders of the deep sea and the splendor of foreign worlds. Whatever is worth learning in the realm of visible things, from the microscopic Infusoria in the drop of water to the most colossal works of man and of nature, all can be made interesting and stimulating in the moving

This first article appeared in *The Cosmopolitan*, 60, no. 1 (December 15, 1915): 22–32. This article was accompanied by several photographs both of Münsterberg and of images from movies used to illustrate the editing and dramatic principles he is explaining. Several of these, with the original captions, appear after page 182. It may have been the first time photographs were used to explain cinematic principles.

The Cosmopolitan Editor's Note: Professor Münsterberg is a wizard at telling us why we do things. He is the first psychologist to take up the study of the strong appeal of the photoplay, and his important conclusions and discoveries here given are quite as interesting and fascinating as those which have proved so helpful in commerce, industry, education, medicine, law, and other spheres of practical life. Very few of the thousands who yield to the lure of the films have any idea that they are more than a substitute for the drama, whereas they are a form of expression entirely foreign to the real stage, and their emotional effects are in some ways quite different from those which we derive from the theater. Doctor Münsterberg points out the direction in which the photoplay must be developed in order to make it the art–expression of the future.

films. Millions have learned in the dark houses their geography and history and natural science.

Yet this power of the moving pictures to supplement the school-room and the newspaper and the library is, after all, much less important than its chief task—to bring entertainment and enjoyment and happiness to the masses. The theater and the vaudeville and the novel must yield room—and ample room—to the art of the pictures.

But can we really say that the film brings us art in the higher sense of the word? Was it not for quite a while the fashion among those who love art to look down upon the tricks of the film and to despise them as inartistic? Those who could afford to visit the true theater felt it as below their level to indulge in such a cheap substitute which lacked the glory of the stage with spoken words. But that time lies far behind us. Even the most artistic public has learned to enjoy a high-class photoplay.

I may confess frankly that I was one of those snobbish late-comers. Until a year ago I had never seen a real photoplay. Although I was always a passionate lover of the theater, I should have felt it as un-dignified for a Harvard Professor to attend a moving-picture show, just as I should not have gone to a vaudeville performance or to a museum of wax figures or to a phonograph concert. Last year, while I was travelling a thousand miles from Boston, I and a friend risked see-ing *Neptune's Daughter*, and my conversion was rapid. I recognized at once that here marvelous possibilities were open, and I began to explore with eagerness the world which was new to me. Reel after reel moved along before my eyes—all styles, all makes. I went with the crowd to Anita Stewart and Mary Pickford and Charles Chaplin; I saw Pathé and Vitagraph, Lubin and Essanay, Paramount and Majestic, Universal and Knickerbocker. I read the books on how to write sce-narios; I visited the manufacturing companies, and, finally, I began to experiment myself. Surely I am now under the spell of the "movies" and, while my case may be worse than the average, all the world is somewhat under this spell.

A NEW FORM OF ART

Why did this change come? Was it because the more and more improved technique brought the imitation of the theater nearer and nearer to the impression of the real stage and thus made the substitute almost as good as the original? Not at all. The real reason was just the opposite. The more the photoplays developed, the more it was felt that it was not their task simply to be an inexpensive imitation of the theater, but that they should bring us an entirely new form of art. As long as the old belief prevailed that the moving-picture performances were to give us the same art which the drama gave, their deficiencies were evident. But if they have an original task, if they offer an art of their own, different from that of the theater, as the art of the painter is different from that of the sculptor, then it is clear that the one is not to be measured by the other. Who dares to say that the marble bust is a failure because it cannot show us the colors which give charm to the portrait painting? On the contrary, we destroy the beauty of the marble statue as soon as we paint the cheeks of a Venus.

It is never the purpose of an art simply to imitate nature. The painting would not be better if the painted flowers gave us fragrance. It is the very essence of art to give us something which appeals to us with the claims of reality and yet which is entirely different from real nature and real life and is set off from them by its artistic means. For this reason we put the statue on a pedestal and the painting into a frame and the dramatic play on a stage. We do not want them to be taken as parts of the real world, and the highest art of all, music, speaks a language which has not even similarity to the happenings of the world.

If the aim of every art were simply to come as near as possible to reality, the photoplay would stand endlessly far behind the performances of real actors on the stage. But when it is recognized that each art is a particular way of suggesting life and of awaking interest, without giving life or nature themselves, the moving pictures come into their own. They offer an entirely new approach to beauty. They give an art which must develop in paths quite separate from those of the stage. It will reach the greater height the more it learns to free itself from the shackles of the theater and to live up to its own forms.

It is only natural that it began with a mere imitation of the theater, just as the automobiles were at first simple horse-carriages moved by machinery. Any new principle finds its own form slowly. The photoplay of today is already as different from those theater imitations as a racing automobile is from a buggy. As soon as the two forms of art are recognized as belonging to two entirely different spheres, they do not disturb each other. Even the most ideal moving picture can never in the least give that particular artistic pleasure which a dramatic theater performance offers. But, on the other hand, even the best drama on the stage will not replace the photoplay as soon as this has reached its ideal perfection.

TRUE MEANING OF THE PHOTOPLAY

What is the true meaning of the "movies"? What are their special ways of showing us the world? In the beginning, the public enjoyed simply the surprising tricks of a technique which showed actual movement in a photograph. But this purely technical interest has long since faded away. What remains, then, as the lasting source of enjoyment? The color is lacking and so is the depth of the stage; above all, the tone of the voice is absent. Yet we do not miss the color, the depth, or the words. We are fully under the spell of this silent world, and the Edison scheme of connecting the camera with the graphophone, and so to add spoken words to the moving pictures, was not successful for very good reasons. It really interfered with the chance of the moving pictures to develop their original nature. They sank back to the level of mere mechanical imitation of the theater.

But while so much was taken away from the offering of every theater stage, how much has come instead! The most evident gain of the new scheme is the reductions of expenses. One actor is now able to entertain a hundred and a thousand audiences at the same time; one stage-setting is sufficient to give pleasure to millions. The theater is thus democratized. Everybody's purse allows him to see the greatest artists, and in every village a stage can be set up. With twenty thousand picture-theaters in this country alone, the hope that the bliss of art may come to everyone has been fulfilled.

But this mere spreading over the globe is not in itself an enrichment of the artistic means. The graphophone brings music into every cottage, but no one can claim that the musical disks have brought us a new art. Their rendering of orchestra or opera is nothing but a mechanical repetition of the free musical art and does not add anything to the symphony or the song.

With the photoplay it is entirely different. It shows us far more than any stage can show, or, rather, it shows us something fundamentally different. The first step away from the theater was soon made. The moving pictures allow a rapidity in the change of scenes which no stage manager could imitate. At first, these possibilities were used only for humorous effects. We enjoyed the lightening quickness with which we could follow the eloper over the roofs of the town, up-stairs and down, into cellar and attic, and jump with him into the motor-car and race over the country roads, changing the background a score of times in a few minutes, until the culprit falls over a bridge into the water and is caught by the police.

This slap-stick humor has not disappeared, but the rapid change of scenes has meanwhile been put into the service of much higher aims. The true development of an artistic plot has been brought to possibilities which the real drama does not know by allowing the eye to follow the hero and heroine continuously from place to place. Now he leaves his room, now we see him passing along the street, now he enters the house of his beloved, now he is led into the parlor, now she is hurrying to the library of her father, now they all go to the garden. New stage-settings are ever sliding into one another; the limitations of space are overcome. It is as if the laws of nature were overwhelmed and, through this liberation from space, a freedom gained which gives new wings to the artistic imagination. This perfect independence from the narrow ties of space-reality gives to the photoplay a new life-chance which alone would secure it the right of a new form of art.

But with the quick change of background, the photoartist also gained the power of a rapidity of motion which leaves actual men behind. And from here it was only a step to the performance of actions which could not be carried out in nature at all. This, too, was made serviceable at first to a rather rough humor. The policeman who climbed up the solid stone front of a high building was in reality photographed creeping over a flat picture of a building spread on the floor. Every day brought us new tricks. We saw how the magician breaks one egg after another and takes out of each egg a little fairy and puts one after another on his hand and how they begin to dance. For the camera, such magical wonders are not difficult, but no theater could ever try to match them. Rich artistic effects are secured, and while on the stage every fairy-tale is clumsy and hardly able to create an illusion, in the film we really see the man transformed into a beast and the flower into a girl.

THE CLOSE-UP

But while, through this power to break down the barriers of space and to make the impossible actions possible, new fascinating effects could be reached, the whole still remained in the outer framework of the stage, inasmuch as everything was the presentation of an action in its successive stages. The photoplay showed a performance, however rapid or impossible, as it would go on in the outer world. An entirely new perspective was opened when the managers of the film-play introduced the "close-up" and similar new methods. The close-up, first made familiar to every friend of the photoplay by the Vitagraph artists, is indeed most characteristic of the emancipation of the moving pictures. As everybody knows, this is the scheme by which a particular part of the picture, perhaps only the face of the hero or his hand or only a ring on his finger, becomes greatly enlarged and replaces, for an instant, the whole stage.

But while everyone is familiar with the method, too few are aware that here indeed we have crossed a great aesthetic line of demarcation and have turned to a form of expression which is entirely foreign to the real stage. Even the most wonderful creations, the great historical plays, where thousands fill the battle-fields, or the most fantastic caprices, where fairies fly over the stage, could be performed in a theater. But this close-up leaves all stagecraft behind. The stage can give us only changes in the outer world; but if we suddenly neglect everything in the room and look only at the hand which carries the dagger, the change is not one outside but inside our mind. It is a turning of our attention. We withdraw our attention from all which is unimportant and concentrate it on that one point on which the action is focussed. The photoplay is an art in which not only the outer events but our own inner actions become effective. Our own attention is projected into the life around us.

NOVEL METHODS OF PRESENTATION

But attention is not the only function of our mind which becomes effective in the moving pictures. Let us think of another action of our mind, the act of memory. When we go through an experience in practical life, we are constantly remembering happenings of the past. The photoplay can overcome the limits of time just as easily as those of space. In many of the newer plays, an unusual fascination is secured by interrupting the pictures of the present events with quickly passing images of earlier scenes. It is as if a quick remembrance were flitting through our mind.

Two passengers are sitting in the smoking-room of a ship; we see them talking about their adventurous life-experiences. The one makes the gesture of speaking; in the next instant we see him climbing the glacier, and then crossing the jungle and shooting tigers, and then fighting in the Boer War, and then strolling through Paris; but every few seconds we return to the smoking-room and keep thus the background of the story before us. Yet our mind does not only combine memories; our thought wanders from one event to another which runs parallel. Here is a dancing-hall in which a man and a girl are flirting; the girl's mother sits at home in a modest attic room and waits for her anxiously; the man's wife is unhappy in her luxurious parlor. Now the three scenes are interwoven: the dancing-hall is seen for ten seconds, then the attic scene for five seconds, the parlor scene for five seconds, then the dancing-hall again, and so on. They chase one another like the tones of an orchestra.

The order of the pictures on the screen is no longer the order of events in nature, but rather that of our own mental play. Here lies the reason why this new art has such peculiar interest for the psychologist. It is the only visual art in which the whole richness of our inner life, our perceptions, our memory, and our imagination, our expectation and our attention can be made living in the outer impressions themselves. As long as the photoartist made no use of these possibilities, his play lagged far behind that of the real theater. But since he has conquered these new methods of mental interpretation, he has created an art which is a worthy rival of the drama, entirely independent from and in not a few respects superior to the theater.

As soon as the original character of the photoplay is understood, it can easily be grasped that we are only at the beginning of a great aesthetic movement. The technical development of the photo-stage and of the camera will go on, and yet that is entirely secondary to the much more essential progress of the new art toward its highest fulfillment. The producer of the photoplays must free himself more and more from the idea with which he started to imitate the stage—and must more and more win for the new art its own rights. How reluctant as yet, for instance, are the efforts to introduce the power of the imagination! In many a photoplay the murderer sees the ghost of his victim. But such devices are, after all, not unfamiliar on the regular stage. Just here the possibilities of the camera are unlimited. The girl in her happy first love sees the whole world in a new glamour and a new radiant beauty. The poet can make her speak so; only the photoplay could show her in this new jubilant world. This is something very different from the charming plays which we already possess today in which Princess Nicotina bewitches us or Neptune's daughter arises from the waves. Such fantastic plays tell us a pretty story, but what we must expect from the photoplay of the future is that the pictures reveal to us our own imaginative play as music can do with its magic tones.

From an artistic point of view, it is entirely wrong to fancy that such imaginative molding of the world must be confined to fairy-tales because it does not correspond to the reality of the world. As long as we argue from such a point of view we have not reached true art. Even the most realistic art always gives us something different from reality. As long as the artistic means harmonizes with our inner view of an experience, it is welcome in the world of art. Even the most rapturous flights of the imagination projected on the screen may have as much inner truth as any melodramatic story. The photoartist needs only the courage to make the spectator feel that he is truly in a temple of art.

HOW THE FILM EXPRESSES EMOTIONS

But even memory, attention, and imagination do not tell the whole story of our inner mind. The core of man lies in his feelings and emotions. As soon as the photoplay moves along its own way, the expression of feelings and emotions will come to the foreground. Of course the producer would say that he shows love and hate and fear and delight and envy and disgust and hope and enthusiasm all in his reels. Certainly he shows them, but simply with the methods of the ordinary stage. The angry man clenches his fist and the frightened man shows signs of terror. We see the gestures and the actions; and yet how inferior is all that to the emotional words which the dramatist can put into the mouth of his persons on the stage! What Romeo and Juliet have to express is, after all, better said by Shakespeare's words than by any mere gestures of tenderness. As long as the photoplay works only with the methods of the theater, we must regret that we are deprived of the words.

But what a different perspective is opened if we think of the unlimited means with which the film may express feeling and sentiment through means of its own. We saw that, in the close-up, the camera can do what in our mind our attention is doing; the camera goes nearer to the object and thus concentrates everything on one point. In our feelings and emotions, the mind takes a sort of stand toward the surroundings. Again, the camera must be made to imitate such a mental action. In the excited mind, the smooth flow of impressions is interrupted. Let the camera break the flow of the pictures. Give us a thought-effect which the musician calls "staccato." We can produce it in the film by omitting certain pictures so that the action seems to jump from one stage to another. Or let the pictures vibrate. We can do this by quickly reversing the order of the pictures which follow one another with the rapidity of sixteen photograms to the second. After pictures 1, 2, 3, 4, 5, 6, we give once more 6, 5, 4, turn then from 4 to picture 9, go back from 9 to 6, then from 6 to 12, and the effect will be that a trilling, vibrating motion goes through the surroundings. Or let the camera turn the straight lines into curves, or the rhythm slow down like a musical adagio, or become rapid like an allegro or presto. In every case effects are produced in which changes of inner excitement seem to take hold of the surrounding world.

IMITATING MENTAL ACTION

The violinist may play one piece after another and we may see in the film the sentiments of those various pieces through the melodious movements around him. His own face may remain unchanged, but everything around him may enter into the mood of the tones and chords. It is in the spirit of the theater to express horror by the wild gestures of the body. It would be in the spirit of the photoplay to make the world around the terrified person change in a horrifying, ghastly way. The camera can do that, and the spectator would come deeply under the spell of the emotion to be expressed. It becomes his emotion, just as in the close-up it is his attention which is forced on the single detail. If a man is hypnotized in the scene, the change of his feelings can only clumsily be shown in his face, but his surroundings may take uncanny forms until a kind of hypnotic spell lies over the whole audience.

Of course the general public would need slowly to be educated toward the higher and higher forms of the photoplayers' art. The masses prefer Sousa's Band to the Boston Symphony Orchestra. It needs a certain training to appreciate the highest forms of art, but nobody doubts that the symphony program, from Beethoven to Debussy, stands on a much higher artistic level that the marches and dances which the unmusical hearers love best. The straight melodrama of the film, offering nothing which the drama of the theater could not present better, will attract the "unmusical" minds more than the true high art of the photoplay. But he who believes the message of beauty for the masses of the people will not yield to such superficial desires. He will unceasingly lift the photoplay to higher and higher art, and to do so he must become conscious of the principles which are involved. But this can be done only if he breaks with the tradition of the theater and understands that the photoplay expresses the action of the mind as against the mere action of the body. Of course the drama presents this inner side of the spoken word which is missing in the pantomime of the film. The inner mind which the camera exhibits must lie in those actions of the camera itself by which space and time are overcome and attention, memory, imagination, and emotion are impressed on the bodily world.

The photoplay of the future, if it is really to rise to further heights, will thus become more than any other art the domain of the psychologist who analyzes the working of the mind. We have seen in recent years how the work of the modern psychologist has become influential and helpful in many different spheres of practical life. Education and medicine, commerce and industry, law and social reform have been greatly aided by the contact with the psychologist, who has put the results of his psychological laboratory into the service of daily life. In the film-world, the only scientist who has been consulted in the past has been the physicist, who prepared the technical devices for the work of the camera. The time seems ripe for his scientific brother, the psychologist, to enter the field and to lead the photoplay to those wonders which its progress has begun to suggest since the leaders dared to leave the paths of mere theatrical performance. The more psychology enters into the sphere of the moving pictures, the more they will be worthy of an independent place in the world of true art and become really a means of cultural education to young and old. The presentations of the films will never supersede those of the theater any more than sculpture can supersede painting or lyrics can supersede music, but they will bring us the noble fulfillment of an artistic desire which none of the other arts can bring.

This is truly the art of the future.

Professor Münsterberg in the Psychological Laboratory, Harvard University.

ty.
lts
1

s
as
ish
il a
never
o-play.
always a
f the thea-
ve felt it as
Harvard profes-
oving-picture show,
not have gone to a

Anita Stewart tells
Doctor Münsterberg
some of her experiences

Anita Stewart tells Doctor Münsterberg some of her experiences as a movie actress.

Scene
from a photo-
play followed by
a "close-up" (below)
This method, first used by the Vitagraph
artists, concentrates the attention upon the
particular object or point on which the
action is focused by allowing it to fill the
screen for an instant. It causes a change
not outside but inside the mind.

tures, was not suc-
cessful for very
good reasons.
It really
inter-
fered with
the chance
of the mov-
ing pictures
to develop
their original
nature. They
sank back to the
level of a mere me-
chanical imitation of
the theater.

But while so much was
taken away from the offering of every theater stage,
how much has come instead!
The most evident gain of the
new scheme is the reduction of

every village a
stage can be set
up. With twenty
thousand picture-theaters
in this country alone, the hope
that the bliss of art may come to
everyone has been fulfilled.

But this mere spreading over the globe
is not in itself an enrichment of the artistic
means. The graphophone brings music

Scene from a photoplay followed by a "close-up" (below). This method, first used by Vitagraph artists, concentrates the attention upon the particular object or point on which the action is focusing by allowing it to fill the screen for an instant. It causes a change not outside but inside the mind.

185

With the photo-play it
s entirely different. It
hows us far more than
ny stage can show, or,
ather, it shows us some-
hing fundamentally dif-
erent. The first step
way from the theater
vas soon made. The
moving pictures allow
a rapidity in the change
of scenes which no stage-
manager could imitate.
At first, these possibilities were used only for
humorous
effects. We
enjoyed the
lightning quick-

Actors and operators in the Pathé photo-play
Creighton Hale and Sheldon Lewis. The

minutes, until the culprit falls
bridge into the water and is

Actors and operators in the Pathé Photoplay studio. In the right foreground we see
Pearl White, leading woman, opposite Arnold Daly, leading man. Standing behind are

place. Now he leaves his room, now we see passing along the street, now he enters house of his beloved, now he is led into

perfect independence from the narrow ties of space-reality gives to the photo-play a new life-chance which alone would secure

Creighton Hale and Sheldon Lewis. The seated figures in the extreme foreground are (left) Theodore W. Warton and (right) Leopold D. Wharton of the Pathé Company.

created an art which is a worthy rival of the drama, entirely independent from and in not a few respects superior to the theater.

As soon as the original character of the photo-play is understood, it can easily be grasped that we are only at the beginning of a great esthetic movement. The technical development of the photo-stage and of the camera will go on, and yet that is entirely secondary to the much more essential progress of the new art toward its highest fulfilment. The producer of photo-plays must free himself more and more from the idea with which he started—to imitate the stage—and must more and more win for the new art its own rights. How reluctant as yet, for instance, are the efforts to introduce the power of imagination! In many a photo-play the murderer sees

WHERE THE PHOTOPLAY
HAS THE ADVANTAGE OVER THE STAGE DRAMA

One important characteristic of the photoplay is that the imagination and other functions of our inner life are presented as external impressions. In this scene, a young girl, surrounded by gay companions, is disturbed by a sudden vision of her lonely mother writing at home. Immediately a picture of the mother and her condition in life is thrown on the screen. It is the development of such possibilities of presentation as here described that will bring the photoplay to its highest perfection.

METHOD OF PRESENTATION
POSSIBLE ONLY IN THE PHOTOPLAY

It is called "switching there and back." The top picture shows an attack with machine guns. The next gives us the effect of the first shots; then we are switched back to a closer view of the firing and finally, in the bottom of the picture, we perceive the results of the continued attack.

formance. The more psychology ↄ
into the sphere of the moving
tures, the more they will
worthy of an independent
in the world of true art
become really a mea
cultural education
young and old.
presentations of the
will never sup
those of the t
any more than
ture can su
painting or lyri
supersede
but they will
us the noble
ment of an a
desire which n
the other art
bring.
This is truly t
of the future.

The photo-play has many ways of awaking interest. Here we see a wife looking from her window—

in the past has been the physicist, who prepared the technical devices for the work of the camera. The time seems ripe for his scientific brother, the psychologist, to enter the field and to lead the photo-play to those wonders which its progress has begun to suggest since the leaders dared to leave the

The photoplay has many ways of awaking interest. Here we see a wife looking from her window—immediately we are shown what the wife observes.

Peril to Childhood in the Movies

Hugo Münsterberg

We have today more than twenty thousand moving-picture theaters in the United States, and every year three billion people pay their nickels and dimes at the entrance gates.

It is claimed that more than a fourth of these spectators are children. Hence, every single day about two million American boys and girls sit for hours in a dark hall and gaze at the pictures on the screen.

The question, accordingly, is not whether our children ought to go to the photoplays. They do go, and the problem is, how can we make sure that this eagerly sought entertainment is a help and not a harm to young minds?

It would be a pitiful wrong if we simply took it for granted that all is right because our boys and girls have a splendid time when they see Mary Pickford or Charlie Chaplin. And it would be no less wrong if we tried to exclude the children from the picture show because some chances of danger threatens.

Our real duty is to recognize in those twenty-thousand theaters a most important educational problem which needs the conscientious study of the social student and the earnest thought of every mother and father.

It would be reckless indeed to ignore the dangers which lurk in

The article first appeared as Hugo Münsterberg, "Peril to Childhood in the Movies," *Mother's Magazine*, 12 (February 12, 1917): 109–110 and 158–9.

Mother's Magazine Editor's Preface: This sensational article is of the first importance because the amazing truths in it, which throw a new light upon the influence that moving pictures have upon the child, have behind them the authority of one of the world's great scientists who presents the results of his own investigations and the significance of them.

the gaudy cinematographic shows. The only peril of which the public is usually aware is the immoral, vicious, and criminal character of too many of the exhibitions. The plays poison the innocent minds and carry the germs of vice and crime into honest homes.

It was this fear which started the demand for rigid censorship of the films. But here we stand before a very complex and vexing question. It may be rather superficial to throw the immoral plays together with the pictures of crime.

No doubt, every year hundreds of photoplays are brought to the market which depict the sins of the senses and unveil the degradation of love. But it may be doubtful whether these dramas of temptation and perversion are really dangerous. Their unclean and suggestive influence may work havoc on the adolescent, but the young child looks on them without understanding.

We are too easily inclined to think that boys and girls see the world with our eyes; their eyes do not notice those moral abysses which we perceive. They see the beautifully dressed women in passionate actions, but as words are missing and as no real indecency is possible in the theater, the clean child remains unaware of the sinister meaning.

Knowledge of the world is needed to interpret the so-called immoral plays as immoral; the ignorance of the normal child is the most effective censor. It seems improbable that the imagination of a wholesome child will be polluted by this influence. Unsavory books, bad company, and even well-intended sexual education draws the fancy into the dangerous paths. But even the worst vampire pictures of the film are fairly harmless to the child. It is half-maturity which needs protection.

It is quite different with the plays which hinge on crime. The theft, the burglary, the murder, are perfectly clear to the young spectators. They understand them just as well as any adult in the audience. Moreover, the effect of such wrongs on their easily molded minds is much stronger than the impression on grown-up people.

The adult has sufficient knowledge of the world to resist the suggestiveness of the wicked deed; the child is fascinated by its romantic surface, by its boldness or cleverness, and from here it is only one step to the impulse to imitate the transgressor.

It has been claimed that more than two-thirds of the juvenile criminals in certain large cities have been found the victims of the moving-picture shows. That is most probably exaggerated; the discovery that a young offender has seen crime depicted on the screen is not sufficient to prove that the one was the cause of the other. But certainly the harmful effect is widespread, and while the immoral picture shows sometimes announce, less for morality than for advertisement's sake, that children will not be admitted, parents ought rather to prevent the attendance of children where the skillful or the daring crime may enrapture their fancy.

ROLE OF CRIME IN MOVIES NOT RESULTS OF CHANCE

Yet we must not forget that this great role which crime plays in the film drama is not a result of chance; it is an organic weakness of the average photoplay. By its lack of words it is inclined to neglect all those subtle shades of feeling and reflection which the story or the drama on the stage allow. Hence it is forced to be satisfied with the coarser emotions and outer actions. And this naturally leads the routine scenario writer to the clumsy scheme of giving undue space to all kinds of crime; they furnish dramatic interest without the need of delicate tracing of the inner life.

Yet we must not think solely of sin and crime if we want to discover the sources of harm and danger. Each single photoplay may be decent and harmless and yet the mental development of the child may be seriously interfered with by the frequent attendance at those shows which are usually offered. Perhaps the worst feature is the utter triviality and cheapness of most photoplays.

The cultural level on which they move is that of the gossiper. The truly relevant elements of social life are disregarded; the humor is farcical, the conflicts are unnatural, the sidelights are those of uncritical reflection. All the well-known regrettable features of the lower type of newspapers are repeated in exaggerated form.

The mind easily becomes accustomed to such an atmosphere of vulgarity and triviality, just as man becomes adjusted to poor air; but this does not contradict the demand of hygiene for fresh air and good ventilation.

Too many evils in the life of the community result from a certain flabbiness of the intellect and indifference of the heart. Among people who have been nourished with gossip in their youth and have not grown up in contact with serious interests, the desire for truth and morality is faint; selfish longings are paramount, graft and corruption flourish and the voice of reform remains unheard.

It has been claimed that the men and women of a community fall into two distinct groups: those who as children grew up in a home with a well-selected little library and those who never had such a privilege. There is probably a core of truth in it; the boy or girl who has been in steady contact with good books from childhood will feel the blessing of it throughout life.

But it is still more true that the steady contact with trash gives the stamp of lasting mediocrity. Just as the hearing of much slang ruins the sense for the subtle shades of language, the seeing of stupid and silly photoplays destroys the finer and deeper values of existence.

We may go still further. The rapid flight of the pictures accustoms the mind to haste and superficiality. The theater play moves slowly from one scene to another and the spoken words carry the mind with deliberate repose from one situation to the next.

But in the "movies" we rush from one place to a dozen others; get only glimpses everywhere; never have time to think about a social problem or conflict which the scene suggests, and while the adult may enjoy the lightening-like rapidity of this change, the child acquires from it the habit of mental haste and carelessness. Instead of the fine discipline of the soul which ought to be the noblest product of the years of education, a trend towards loose, shiftless thinking and acting must result.

MOST OF PICTURES DRAG OUT STORY TO RIDICULOUS LENGTH

Yet in spite of all this haste, most of the moving pictures today do not even tell their story quickly: on the contrary, by introducing an abundance of trivial matter they are often spun out to ridiculous length. A plot sufficient for a short play is often drawn out into five reels and as in most houses a new play begins in a tasteless fashion a few seconds after the close of the last, the child is lured into staying for hours. It is too often a waste of time which interferes with better methods of spending leisure hours.

Finally, while all this is true with regard to the healthy and normal child, much more might be added with regard to the weak and nervous youngster. The flickering which is fatiguing to the eyes of many sound spectators must be a severe strain to the eyes of nervous children, and the long stay in the dark auditorium may produce a dangerous irritation. The unreal, exaggerated emotionalism of most melodramatic photoplays naturally increases this danger for excitable nerves.

The accusations sound so formidable that it seems that only one decision would be reasonable: boys and girls must be kept away from the photoplay houses under all circumstances. We taboo the saloon and the cigarets for the child: why not the "movies"?

MAY WASTE TIME IN PICTURE SHOWS, BUT IS OFF THE STREET

Why do not the educators implore the parents in city and village strictly to forbid the pictures which lure the children into their treacherous labyrinth?

But to do so would be shortsighted and inexcusable. It would mean to overlook the tremendous amount of good which the screen theater may bring to every child. It would mean to ignore that the moving pictures may be a public school with splendid influence on every girl and boy.

There is indeed another side to every one of our objections. Surely a child may waste much of his time in the nickel show, but is there not a great chance that the boy who sees with eager eyes and throbbing heart the wonders of the film, otherwise would spend the time on the street, perhaps in bad company? After all, no small service is done to the community if an entertainment is offered which for a most modest price holds the unruly youth spellbound through long leisure hours which otherwise might be misused.

Yet it would be poor praise if nothing better could be said about the picture places than that they keep their little patrons out of mischief. A true welcome can be given them only if they themselves bring valuable elements into the life of the child.

But they do bring such enrichment abundantly. The motion pictures are, first of all, great teachers of knowledge. Every feature of the wide world can be brought near to the youthful imaginations. No more patient, no more amiable, no more persuasive teacher could be found.

Whatever the child may learn about mankind and about nature in the schoolroom—history and geography, zoology and botany, and what not—might be translated into a fascinating lesson for the eye. And in its moving form it impresses the young mind more strongly than any verbal description or any simply printed illustration could do.

Many moving-picture companies have specialized in these educational regions and have brought to the market an ample supply of beautiful, instructive pictures which any intelligent boy or girl would enjoy. They lead the child far beyond the horizon of the regular school lesson.

The whole development of the human race from the lowest life of the savages to the thousandfold forms of modern civilization all over the globe is made alive. The child sees the manifoldness of human ways, of foreign customs and life, of forms of art and architecture and works of technique in distant lands, of characteristic landscapes near and far as backgrounds of other peoples.

The great events which have been given new turns to history are dramatized; Greece and Rome, the medieval days and the glories of recent centuries appeal to the child in the interesting settings of the past.

Explorers and adventurers lead him to the remotest corners of the earth, naturalists to the queerest and rarest species among plants and animals; the wonders of the deep sea, the secrets of the jungle are disclosed.

Yes, the camera makes him see what no human eye can observe in reality, the growth of flowers and beasts. In a few seconds the orchid grows up and blossoms and unfolds its flowers, or the caterpillar creeps over the twig and spins its cocoon and breaks it as a butterfly— on the film, events are recorded together which fill weeks and months in nature.

But the educational pictures offer still other avenues to useful knowledge. The children may learn to understand the industries and institutions which surround them. They are brought into the factories and mills, to the fields and ranches and mines, to the centers of commerce and public life, to court-rooms and hospitals and legislatures; they see the current events in all the States. Truly whoever wants to learn has wonderful chances.

Yet it would be one-sided if we were to think only of the so-called educational films as sources of knowledge. No doubt, many a boy and girl has an instinctive dislike for such outspoken pedagogical means. When they go to enjoy themselves they do not want to feel that pictorial schoolbooks are forced on them. The managers of the playhouses have taken the hint and the result is that the films, which are made solely for instruction's sake, are not so frequently offered as they deserve. But does that mean that the children are deprived of every opportunity to get new information from the performances? Certainly not. Every good and interesting photoplay, however far it may be from the direct aims of the teachers, may teach the young mind much which may not be learned so easily in other ways. The child looks there into many new varieties of human society and widens his horizon steadily.

Even for the adult it is true that the more significant photoplays give him plenty of chance to see new aspects the community; he may get a clearer insight into the social existence in the slums or in certain industries than he probably would get by practical contact. This holds still more for the boy and girl.

The city child sees how the villager lives, and the child of the hamlet gets glimpses of city life. They see the landscape and the life of foreign lands, and above all, the inmost features of the various callings and vocations. Every background, every interior can become a realistic lesson.

The child begins to understand the energies which are at work in the community. Many a journey through the country and many a pilgrimage through the homes and workshops of the people would be needed to open such varied vistas of the life into which the adolescent will have to enter.

But the young mind has to learn more than facts. No lesson is more needed than that of wholesome emotion and pure feeling and sentiment.

The moral education is still more important than the intellectual; what an inspiration and genuine cultivation of the heart may be won in those thrilling hours in front of the screen. Noble ambition for highest life work, sympathy with the sufferer, distaste for the unclean, contempt for the dishonest, may be developed; a high-minded patriotism may be kindled; enthusiasm for everything great and upbuilding may be stirred in the mind throughout those most formative years of youth.

The emotional influence of the photoplay, however, which is the most direct, and therefore the strongest, is the artistic one. Every photoplay ought to carry the messages of real beauty; the beauty of the plot as literary art; the beauty of high-class acting as dramatic art; the beauty of the pictures as fine art.

Nothing is more needed by the youth of the country than the inner adjustment to the ideals of beauty. The life which surrounds them is too full of harsh, practical interests; too much is controlled by mere commercial selfishness and ugly strife. We need more of the spirit of harmony and devotion to ideals. We need the teaching of beauty implanted early in every heart.

Few children have the good fortune to hear good music and to see fine paintings and to attend artistic theater performances. The photoplay is the only art with high artistic possibilities which really reaches the millions during their schooltime. Has the nation the right to neglect this tremendous opportunity?

No, we cannot and ought not to keep away the youth from these sources of wider knowledge, of moral uplift and of inspiring beauty. And yet, we must not forget for a moment all those dangers and risks which we recognized. Hence, our duty is clear: we must take care that the good features of the photoplays are fully utilized for the development of our boys and girls, and that the harmful features are at the same time sternly suppressed by the sound sense of the community.

The decisive step probably must be a rigid demand that in the large cities special kinematoscopic theaters for the youth be maintained, and that in smaller towns special children's performances be regular features of the program.

The children can get real advantage only from photoplays and pictures which are different from those which the adult public expects. It is not enough to separate the performances for the children simply by announcing that boys and girls are admitted at an especially low entrance price. The essential feature is rather that the program be carefully adjusted to the needs of the child.

The cheapness and lack of originality of the scenarios is the central evil of the whole moving-picture industry today. Millions are spent for gorgeous productions with costly scenery and high-salaried actors and actresses, while all this is built on scenarios written by third-class talents, simply because no honorariums are paid for the scenarios which would draw a first-class writer away from his more lucrative writing of stories and novels and dramatic plays.

The resulting triviality of the scenarios lowers the level of the film art for the adult in an often intolerable way; yet the children have to suffer from it still more severely. The best talent is just good enough to write scenarios which can really upbuild the youth of the country.

As soon as the producing companies understand that the parents and educators feel the need and know what they want, they will adjust themselves to the new request of the public. It could be so easily done; all which is needed is to reduce the ludicrous expenses for the setting and the acting of the performances, and to spend the funds saved for the writing of really valuable scenarios.

Interview with Hugo Münsterberg

Question: Are you interested in the development of the moving pictures?

Münsterberg: I may admit that my interest is of rather recent date, as I had a deep aesthetic prejudice against the drama on the screen and avoided every moving picture house until about a year ago. But since I saw a photoplay for the first time my interest has rapidly grown and I have tried to make quite a serious study of the problem. My little book on *The Photoplay*, which appeared a few weeks ago, is an earnest witness of it with two hundred and thirty pages of evidence. I am sincerely convinced that the moving pictures are destined to a wonderful career of which we see at present only the beginning.

Q: In what direction do you expect the growth? Do you hope for the uplift by educational features?

M: Surely I see most promising possibilities in making the screen useful for educational purposes. I do not mean by that a dry teaching by pictures but an awakening of interests. The rapid pictures cannot replace a thorough study, but they can stimulate the imagination. Hence I welcomed the Paramount Pictograph, which offers the features of a magazine in picture form and was glad to contribute to its articles some psychological experiments by which I could stir up popular interest in the testing of minds for vocational guidance. Yet the fundamental advance for which I hope has to be an artistic one.

Q: Do you consider the moving pictures a real art?

Editor's Note: The following is a transcript of an interview with Hugo Münsterberg from April 25, 1916, conducted by the Paramount Pictures Company. The original copy is in the Münsterberg Papers at the Boston Public Library (MS Acc. 2461). The interview was edited and reprinted in the *New York Dramatic Mirror* on June 3, 1916.

M: Certainly I do, and here I differ most from the popular view which sees in the "movies" merely an inexpensive imitation of the theatre. I am convinced that the photoplay represents an entirely new independent art which can be understood only if the comparison with the theatre is abandoned. The photoplay has its own laws and its own life conditions and is different from the drama of the stage as music is different from literature or painting different from sculpture. To be sure, much must be changed in order that the new art really come to its full expression. The scenarios must be written by men who can better emancipate themselves from the traditions of the theatre. The printed leaders must be more and more discarded. Only the pictures should speak to us.

Q: How do you feel about the music?

M: The musical accompaniment of the photoplays is one of the most urgent questions in the realm of this new art. Until a few months ago the so called music which accompanies the pictures interfered more than any other feature with the true artistic effects of the photoplays. In the poorer houses it was often an atrocious noise which could have ruined even an ideal photoplay, and in the better places it was too often an indifferent music-making which might have been tolerated as accompaniment to a dinner in a restaurant with soft red shades, but it was devoid of all aesthetic significance in a film theatre.

Q: Would it be better then to omit the music altogether?

M: No. That would be no solution of the question. An audience sitting for hours in a darkened hall and engaged only in viewing a dumb show would soon become restless and nervous, and the one sided engagement of the senses would produce intolerable tension. Even if a single individual could stand it, a large audience would get hysterical. The ears must be stimulated somehow or there would soon result a torturing craving for the voices of the actors. The only true solution of the problem is the subtle adjustment of the accompanying music to the pictorial text. No responsible producing company ought to send out a photoplay without making sure that music of their own selection be rendered at the performance, and this selection must not be a routine choice of favorite melodies, but a truly musical interpretation of the play. If the art of the film develops, as I am sure that it can, the time will not be far distant when composers will be glad to bring their talents into the service of the photoplay and write music for it as they now do for the opera. But as long as we have no specially composed accompaniment, it is not difficult to select from the wealth of musical literature characteristic pieces which can be adapted to the needs of any particular play. Different musical schools may take a different stand here as in the opera and in the symphony as to the degree in which the music itself ought to tell the story. The accompaniment may be imitative of the sounds and noises of life and the orchestra may thunder when the lightening flashes in the pictures. Or the music may remain in the limits of purely tonal beauty. In either way the goal can be reached: the mind of the hearer combines the melodies and harmonies with the passing pictures and melts the impressions of the ears with those of the eyes into a unified whole, the parts of which support one another. A cultivated audience simply will not tolerate any longer a performance in which photoactors, who are paid hundreds of thousands a year, play while pianists, whom any Society for the Hygiene of the Ears ought to put behind bars, hammer away at the same time.* But the mere replacing of the piano by an organ is surely not sufficient. The most artistic adjustment of the music to the play is the one condition upon which everything depends. It can be done, and it has been done, but exception must become the rule; and such a change will react favorably on the total world of the film.

---

*I have rewritten this sentence, as it makes no sense in the original manuscript (ed.).

Speech on the Paramount Pictographs

The Paramount reception at the exposition brought together an unusual number of notable people of the screen. An exhibition of George Beban in *Pasquale* was made one afternoon and evening and Mr. Beban was present to give a little talk and receive his friends. Dorothy Dent was the guest of honor at the reception, and Fanny ward came to the Garden to see herself on the screen for the first time in *The Cheat.* Jack Dean, who in private life is Fanny Ward's husband, accompanied her. Burton Holmes and Professor Münsterberg were also present.

Hugo Münsterberg, Harvard psychologist, scenario writer and associate editor of the Paramount Pictographs, spoke at the exposition on how he dared put psychology into motion pictures. He said he realized that the screen provided a more universal textbook than the laboratories could ever become and that psychology might become a vast and far-reaching influence through its presentation on the screen.

"Much is heard about the conservation of natural resources in this country," said Professor Münsterberg. "But what, if anything, is heard about conserving the natural talents of young people, about directing their ability in the proper direction? Practically nothing. Here is where I saw that the Paramount Pictograph might step in to direct a vast wealth of talent into their proper channels."

"I have arranged my mental tests in the Pictograph so that motion picture audiences may learn what characteristics equip one for special kinds of work, so that each individual may find his proper setting. These are tests to show whether one has constructive imagination,

From the article entitled "Münsterberg Speaks at Paramount Reception. George Beban and other Notables at Exposition," *Motography* 15, n. 22 (May 27, 1916): 1215.

the ability to think quickly—these are for the executive type of mind, which must be able to grasp the meaning of a situation as soon as it presents itself. My scenario shows simply how the constructive mind can build names out of letters arranged in a totally different order from the original one."

"For the man who does detail work there is another kind of test. In this the pictures show how keen is one's power of observation and the scenes have important details missing which may not be apparent at first glance. There is no type of mind which cannot be classified through this series, which may do a wonderful work in making the necessary connection between talent and the occupation for which it is best suited."

"While the schoolbooks of the past may not be discarded for the screen, the films will have perhaps a wider and greater field of usefulness. There need be no limits practically to the influence of the motion picture as an educator, although there is no subject which can be more clearly presented through the camera than psychology."

Index

1424